"I believe those who rea
in love to be real and po
than we can think to ask
the way to Jesus where l
anyone living this life."

Lynn Tredway
Oakdale, CA

"Diane is a reliable, wise and thoughtful guide through the dark
journey of deep grief. If you have lost a loved one, this book will
not only resonate with you, you will also find a life-giving
companion in Diane and her encouraging words."

Mindy Hedges
Austin, TX

"Many people who enter extreme grief tend toward a process of
denial, followed by a myriad of coping mechanisms that won't
work and don't heal. Diane gives us a model of how to accept and
go through the pain and truly be healed and transformed by God
without spending months and years chained in bondage. No matter
what your experience is with pain, grief, and suffering–this is
proof—**There is Hope for all of us in the Trinity!**"

Aimee D. Harris
Danville, CA

"The advice, tools, and answers in this book are crucial for anyone
going through the tragedy of losing a child or loved one. But the
book not only addresses grief, it also provides valuable survival
skills for anyone trying to live joyfully and purposefully in our
challenging world. **A Highly Recommended Read!**"

Karen Platt
Pleasanton, CA

"Diane has put into words a true story of one of life's pathways
that no one would choose to go down. But it does happen every
day in this life. My brother lived through some of these same
feelings that Diane writes about after losing his own son. Starting
with heart-wrenching grief, my brother also found that life can be
turned around into joy because of God's great love for all of us
through the sacrifice made through His Son. Jesus gives each of us
Hope, even in life's darkest moments."

Debbie LeBlanc
Rockledge, FL

It STARTED *in the* DARK

You don't have to chase healing...
it will find you on the path there.

DIANE C. SHORE

Anything is possible when
you follow the Son!

Publishing

DCShore Publishing
dcshorepublishing.com

ISBN: **0990523101**
ISBN-13: **978-0990523109**

DEDICATION

For you, Jesus, because without You, my Lord, I have nothing. And with You, I have everything I need. You are my eternal Hope! *The Lord is my Shepherd, I shall not want.* Psalm 23 (NKJV)

For you, Philip Andrew Shore, because without you, my son, I might not realize how much I need Jesus. And with you, I will always have a reminder of what Heaven holds for those who will believe. *Blessed are the poor in spirit. For theirs is the kingdom of heaven.* Matthew 5:3 (NKJV)

For you, Charlotte Beyer, because without you, Grandma, I wouldn't have had a lifetime of watching a faith walk through grief. And with you, I have seen that, *weeping may stay for the night, but rejoicing comes in the morning.* Psalm 30:5 (NIV)

I love you more, Phil.

CONTENTS

Have you come to the Red Sea place in your life,

Where, in spite of all you can do,

There is no way out, there is no way back,

There is no other way but through?

Then wait on the Lord with a trust serene

Till the night of your fear is gone;

He will send the wind, He will heap the floods,

When He says to your soul, "Go on."

Red Sea Place
By: Annie Johnson Flint

Please stop here first,
before you enter into the pages of this book!

Did you know that a pansy is also called a Heart's Ease?

My purpose for writing this book was to do just that~put your heart at ease by finding peace through the Hope that Jesus offers us. But I have to warn you, do not mistake ease for easy. This is not an easy read. For most, it will be emotional and challenging. Because of the subject matter, this story needs the bold Truth of Jesus Christ to be presented here.

You may have picked this book up, or been given this book, because your heart is broken. The Truth is, Jesus can help you. But you first have to come to Him, and put your trust in Him. Jesus came to this world over 2,000 years ago to bind up the brokenhearted, and to offer us His Saving Grace. He will also be coming back again one day to take us Home to Heaven. We don't know if that will be in 10, 20, or 30 years, or 10, 20, or 30 minutes. But if Jesus should return, even before you finish reading this book, I pray you will be ready to meet Him. If you're not sure if you are, and would like to be, you might consider reading the last pages of this book first. Haven't you always wanted to do that? Well, here's your chance. I'm encouraging you to. Please turn to page 248 right now. Go ahead and read the Epilogue before you read the Introduction. It's your opportunity to meet Jesus, if you haven't as yet—honestly, it's the only way this book will make any sense.

I pray that no matter what you are going through, you will find some help and comfort within these pages.

Living in Jesus' saving grace,

Diane

Heart's Ease

INTRODUCTION

For if you already have something, you don't need to hope for it.
But if we look forward to something we don't have yet,
we must wait patiently and confidently.
Romans 8:24b-25 (NLT)

It's three o'clock in the morning, and I am wide-awake. This is not normal for me. I am a good sleeper, loving my 8-9 hours of sleep each night. But tonight, I am here writing. Is it God who woke me in the middle of the night? Perhaps. He's been working on an idea in my heart and mind for a new book to write. It's a book that started 12 years ago when our 16 year old son was in the final stages of Leukemia. This is a book that describes the "Me" back then, and the happenings surrounding what it is like to not only help your child through cancer, but also help him to go Home to Heaven after five and one half years of battling it. This book will also contain "Myself" now—the person who has lived through the most devastating event a parent has to face, and has found some of the answers to questions I asked myself along the way. Not only asked myself, but also asked "The Great I AM." I have told people, by the time you understand chemotherapy, you are usually either healed on this earth or healed in Heaven. But the information gathered during that journey can help another just starting theirs. It seems the same with the grief journey. We enter into it not knowing so many things, and needing the help of someone who has gone ahead to show us the way through. It seems that is what I have been called to write, starting officially at three o'clock this morning, July 23, 2013.

Half of this book has already been written before I have even gotten started. It will be taken from the writings that I have done over the past 12 years. I will include portions of those blog messages that went out to family and friends describing each step, each emotion, and each question along the way. I wrote to not only share the journey, but to heal through the journey, and to process all the crazy mixed up and even sometimes lucid thoughts a Mom goes through when seeing the ending of the life of her child on this earth, and the beginning of living a life without her child each day. I knew of no other way to cope but through prayer, God's Word, and writing my way through such difficult years of pain and missing our son. My husband and I also found that by my writing, and his reading, we moved through grief at about the same rate of healing. What I would write, would also help him understand what he was feeling, which was very similar, and once "voiced," it could be dealt with and moved through.

"The only way out is through." A wise man once told me that early on in my grief. He, too, was missing a precious son on this earth. But I didn't really know what those words fully meant when he said them to me. I only began to understand them as I moved through grief myself, knowing just one thing for sure; I DIDN'T want to get STUCK in it! By *it*, I mean the darkness, the pain, the unanswered questions that haunted me along the way. The mind can be the devil's playground if every thought is not taken captive to Christ. That took practice, because there are so many tortuous thoughts in all that has happened that aren't easily dismissed. They run through a grieving brain thousands of times, wondering, and questioning, and agonizing over every little detail that could have been done differently, things that should have been said, things that have been and will be missed. The list is endless, and the thoughts are endless. Most of those thoughts worked their way out of my head and into my prayers, and out through my fingers on a keyboard through the years—if not for anyone else to read, then for my own sanity. And it worked. I'm here today, this day, at three thirty in the morning now to say, "I'm still here. And my heart has stopped hurting. And I have found that life is good again. And it really does get better!" That's what this book will be about; how God can take us from A to Y on this journey of grief. God does have a plan, and it does work! Why only "Y"? Because Z, to me, is being reunited in Heaven with all those who believe that Jesus Christ is our Lord and Savior. That, we are still waiting on.

Do I still miss Phil every day? You bet I do! Our whole family does; and we talk about him and share him with our six grandchildren as much as we share about anyone else in our family. He is still a part of our family, he has just moved on ahead to a wondrous place. We talk about seeing him again, just like any relative that has gone on a glorious trip. The only difference is he won't be coming back to us, but we will be going to him because of the saving grace of Jesus Christ. (2 Samuel 12:23b)

Because of this tremendous trial, I have learned to have a confident hope in God's promises. It is a gift that comes because of the process talked about in Romans 5:3-5 (NLT). *We can rejoice, too, when we run into problems and trials, for we know that they help us develop endurance. And endurance develops strength of character, and character strengthens our confident hope of salvation. And this hope will not lead to disappointment. For we know how dearly God loves us, because he has given us the Holy Spirit to fill our hearts with his love.*

I have learned to endure. It has built in me a new strength of character, which brings about a confident hope of our salvation. I wasn't always this confident. I didn't always understand endurance. And my character had some darker shades of gray. But God and the last twelve years have changed my heart, my mind, and my relationship with our Father in Heaven. How does a person go from questioning to knowing, from doubting to believing, from hurting to healing? That is what we will explore here together as I intertwine the **agony** grief brings, with God's glorious, **healing** ways that can come with time and prayer through the years.

I will be taking what was written by "Me," a grieving Mom, and answer with what I "Myself" have learned through the years from "The Great I AM" by using His Word and every other tool He has given us along the way. I'm not saying I have all the answers, but I have some experience under my belt that may be useful to help another travel their own journey through grief and beyond.

Thank You Lord, for waking me in the dark hours of the night to begin this new writing project. Thank You for planting this idea through my new found friend, Jenn. In writing to her in her grief after saying good-bye to her precious little girl, it seems the archives of pain intertwined with present day healing may be a useful tool for someone else along the way. I don't know what plans You have for this project, I only know I need to be faithful to do what You are calling me to do. You have taught me that obedience brings great joy.

So let's begin with the story containing Me, Myself, and The Great I AM!

Me
2001

Myself
2014

"You cannot see my face, for no one may see me and live."

Exodus 33:20 (NIV)

**The Great
I AM**

CHAPTER ONE

Me

A Smile From Heaven...

(Written in the wee hours of the morning after Philip left us at
10:19 P.M. on Wednesday, November 14, 2001)

Thursday, 15 Nov 2001

*A smile from Heaven shines down on us tonight. Our dear sweet,
Philip has gone Home. Words to express how we're feeling...are
there any? We were with him, and now we're not. He is happier
now than we can imagine, but our hearts are broken. We must get
up in the morning and face the day. Yet his days are never ending,
Phil is at rest. He so longed for that, today especially. God's
timing is perfect in all things. We can't even absorb the reality of
it. That will come, and with it more tears than we can imagine. But
through the tears, we will remember our wonderful son. What a
gift he was and is to us. We will cling to the memories, rejoice in
his life, thank God for each day, and keep following our Savior
until the day He leads us Home where good-byes are not even
spoken.*

Phil liked this verse, so we are sharing it with you.

Philippians 1:18-23(NIV)
Yes, and I will continue to rejoice, for I know that through your prayers and the help given by the Spirit of Jesus Christ, what has happened to me will turn out for my deliverance. I eagerly expect and hope that I will in no way be ashamed, but will have sufficient courage so that now as always Christ will be exalted in my body, whether by life or by death. For to me, to live is Christ and to die is gain. If I am to go on living in the body, this will mean fruitful labor for me. Yet what shall I choose? I do not know. I am torn between the two: I desire to depart and be with Christ, which is better by far...

Thank you so much for all your love, prayers, and support. We can't tell you how much we appreciate all of you in helping us through this time, and the days ahead.

Love, The Shores

Myself

We must get up in the morning and face the day.

And face the day... It is morning now. I did go back to sleep when I finished the beginning of this book. I didn't know if I could sleep, but I prayed, "Help me God. I need to go to sleep." And sleep I did.

Upon waking this morning, I thought about my three o'clock in the morning writing, and I asked God, "Why did You have me get up in the middle of the night to start writing?" It seemed He gently whispered back to me, "It started in the dark." Oh, that seems appropriate. Not only in the actual dark night of November 14, 2001, but with darkness in my soul too. "And rejoicing comes in the morning. Right Lord." So here we go!

Each day now, 12 years later, I start my day "in the light," with the Word of God, my coffee, and a banana. There is hardly a day that I don't open up my now well-worn Bible and seek God's wisdom and a closer relationship with Him. Where did that habit come from? It came from grief, from needing God so badly that I could barely breathe, and from finding out through the years that the air I breathe does come directly from God. The Hope in my heart, on this day, has come from Him. The peace about where Phil is, has come from Heaven above. And I am grateful.

I wake each day now with a thankful heart. I wake knowing that God will get me through this day, one more day of living without Phil. Each day brings me one day **closer** to seeing him again. I also wake knowing it won't be painful like it once was. Oh, there will be times, very few and far between now, when some tears will fill my eyes, and that's okay. I know God doesn't have a problem with tears, because He knows how to wipe them away if we will let Him.

Words to express what we're feeling...are there any?

There have been too many to count through the years. Being the writing type, my words have been collected onto pages; hundreds and thousands of pages. They are there to refer back to. I had no idea how valuable those pages would be, not only to me, but to share with others. God knew. He even had my friend, Lilia, stop by on Phil's last day on earth. She gave me a book. When I started reading it weeks later, I was astounded. It wasn't a book on grief. It was a book about a writer. God seemed to be saying the life I once had with Phil was ending, but a new life of writing was beginning. Only God knew that was Phil's last day on earth. Only God knew I would be here today writing. Even now, I marvel at how God puts the pieces of our lives together.

We can't absorb the reality of it yet.

In the beginning, I wrote of things I had no idea about, **let alone** how they would turn out. There is so much I want to tell you about this journey, but I am holding back, starting slow, just like grief is. It is a very slow, very long, and yet, it can be a very purposeful journey if we so choose. God says He sets before us life and death, and to choose life. There were days when I so wanted to choose life, but some days when the reality set in, death seemed much more welcome.

For to me, to live is Christ and to die is gain. If I am to go on living in the body, this will mean fruitful labor for me. Yet what shall I choose? I do not know! I am torn between the two: I desire to depart and be with Christ, which is better by far...
Philippians 1:21-23 (NIV)

Phil felt that too, the pain of living, and the relief dying could hold for him. We all do, I believe, at certain times in our lives. But we must go on, because God has a purpose for all of our pain, even if we can't see it at the moment. Phil now looks back from his Heavenly Home, from a Heavenly perspective. I can only imagine what that must be like, to see things so clearly, without the fog of the enemy that surrounds us here on earth. To know the full Truth without the lies always milling about trying to deceive our hurting hearts. Grief, if gone through with Jesus, and looked back on, can give us a glimpse of a Heavenly perspective. Grief can take our eyes off of this world and set them on the next. That is a gift grief can give us, if we will allow it to.

Gift #1 – A glimpse of a Heavenly Perspective that eases the burdens of this earth.

Where is your perspective on this day in your own pain?

Where would you like your perspective to be?

Record today's date and other notes you'd like to make:

The Great

I AM

Yes, and I will continue to rejoice, for I know that through your prayers and the help given by the Spirit of Jesus Christ, what has happened to me will turn out for my deliverance.
Philippians 1:18-19 (NIV)

CHAPTER TWO

*Does it mean he no longer loves us if we
have trouble or calamity...?*
Romans 8:35 (NLT)

<u>Me</u>

This Morning

Friday, 16 Nov 2001

*I wake this morning with a pain like I have never felt before. It
doubles me over as the tears pour out. It builds in intensity until I
think I will die myself. I want to touch Phil. I want to hold his
hand, and tell him I love him just one more time. I want to tell him
how much I miss him. Did I hug him enough? Did I tell him how
much we would miss him? Did I let him go too easily? I
encouraged him to go Home—that his job was finished here and
that we would be fine. I told him God would take care of us, just as
He has always done. And now I agonize over releasing Phil
without showing him the suffering that would lie in the aftermath
of his departure. Like he needed to see that? No!*

I asked him to please share with me anything and everything he was going through, because he knew I like to write and I told him someday I may write a book to help others get through these times. Maybe there were others who could not share with each other like he and I could, and that it would be of help to someone else. He was so sweet. He would share whatever he could when he could speak. We talked about so much in the week previous to his leaving, and during that week, he cried more tears than he ever had before as he poured out so many different feelings. I know God was preparing him as he worked through that.

Then on Saturday night, we sat on the edge of his bed as he told me more of how he was feeling, and what he wanted to do. I thanked him for the decisions he was making, so that his dad and I would not have to make them. We would honor his decisions. (I told him he didn't have to eat if he didn't want to. He said he didn't want to. I told him drinking water would probably make him feel better. He said he would drink water.) After talking that Saturday, he was done with most of the tears. He spoke very little. He retreated into himself very peacefully, and just enjoyed the family being around him.

We went to church on Sunday morning; he was in his wheelchair. Then we spent the day together as a family and watched the Raider game. He slowly left us from then on, and we let him. We cared for him, and we read to him. We wiped the sweat off his face, and held his hand. I kissed his cheeks and his forehead, and looked into his eyes many, many times as he would just gaze around the room and at us. Phil was here, in his bed, with us and his dog, and he waited for the "train" to come.

The last night, I was lying in his bed with him, and his breathing was very rapid. He said, "Mom, I know my breathing is bothering you. But really, I'm feeling better; this cold medicine seems to really be working now." I said "Phil, you're not bothering me." He was such a sweet kid. Earlier in the evening he had coughed and then he apologized for not covering his mouth. Oh my. Phil kept mumbling things, but once in awhile I could understand what he was saying. I thought he was hallucinating because I had given him a little morphine to take the edge off his very sore throat. He said, "Mom, I feel like I'm putting everything away. Am I putting things away Mom?" It didn't really need an answer...but I didn't realize until later why he was "putting everything away." Maybe something inside of him knew the time was near, and he was finishing up details in his own head. His breathing became louder and more rapid, and his heart was beating so fast. I thought maybe I should get up and get some of the medication that we had just gotten from the hospice nurse to calm him a bit.

When I walked to his door, Chris (Phil's 20 year old brother) was standing outside it because he had heard the commotion going on. I told him to get Dad, and then I went back to Phil's bedside. Phil looked at me and he said, "Mom, I think God is healing me! I'm really feeling a lot better. I'm going to feel good tomorrow, Mom!" I said, "I love you, Phil," and he said, "I love you." And then Chris and Jim were there. Chris said, "I love you, Phil," and Phil turned to him and said, "I..." and he couldn't say anymore. Chris just put his hand on his forehead and said, "It's okay bud, you don't have to say it." And then he started to leave us and it took about 15 minutes for him to go, and at 10:19 PM he breathed his last.

We said good-bye and told him what a good job he had done, and so many other things. We called younger Jimm (Phil's 23-year-old brother), and our minister to the house. When they got here, we all sat around Phil's bed. We talked and shared stories through the tears, and just spent a very special last hour or so with him. Then we prayed and left his room.

I would go back from time to time while we waited for procedures to be done, and Phil had this smile on his face that I hadn't seen before. Just a little look of "Ahhh, I'm done." Phil was not there, just the body he no longer needed. But he was still my son, and I still kissed him and hugged him tightly. I could, because I no longer had to be concerned about hurting him. The process of dying reminded me of the process of being born. We were there to coach him through, to encourage him, to bring him ice chips, wipe his brow, and he was focused. No glasses on, no TV on, just quiet. We read to him all the verses and messages of love sent to him from family and friends. And we read from his Bible. LOTS of Scripture. Now when we hear those verses, we think, I just read that to Phil.

As I left my room this morning in agony of spirit, I went into his room, laid down on his bed and cried. And then I got up, and knelt by his bed, right where I had been while he was dying. I picked up all the e-mail messages and started to read through them little by little, and they were so comforting to me; to know that these were some of the last words that Phil heard. They helped him, and now they were helping me. I just want you to know that you were all with him, as we were. Although it was a very private time, it was also a shared time with all of you. Thank you, for helping Phil through his "labor" of being born into Heaven.

Now if you don't mind, because writing this is very therapeutic for me, I would still like to share this journey with you for a while—maybe for a long while. Maybe this is how I will write my book. Maybe some of these thoughts are too private and you wonder why I would want to share them. But life and death happen to us all. Why should we not share that? My tears have stopped for a while this morning, and it feels good to work through it "on paper." Will you take this journey with me? Or if you like surprise endings, you could wait until the book comes out. Although, we already know how the story ends—we all live happily after, for "to live is Christ and to die is gain." Phil liked that.
So do I!

Yesterday, we tried not to do too much because we just wanted quiet time to reflect on everything. This has been a very long journey with Phil, and one of the greatest lessons we have learned is to take things one day at a time. We are trying to continue on with what we have learned and not hurry through this process of making arrangements and finishing what has been started.

Philippians 1:6 (NIV) ...he who began a good work in you will carry it on to completion until the day of Christ Jesus.

<u>Myself</u>

I wake this morning with a pain like I have never felt before.

That line makes me inhale, and exhale slowly... I'm SO thankful to not be there anymore. But having been there, I know it. I know it all too well. That pain didn't disappear in a day, a week, a month or even a year. It took time and God to ease what seemed might never go away. But go away, it did. This morning I wake with a peace like I might have never felt if not for having gone through such a deep, dark valley.

So many said, with all good intentions, "I can't imagine." And I would reply, "You really can't, and I don't want you to even try." There were times in Phil's illness when I would "go there" in my thoughts, trying to imagine living without him. What I imagined never even came close to what I felt when I wrote that line twelve years ago.

Did I hug him enough? Did I tell him how much we would miss him? Did I let him go too easily?

If we have ever loved and lost, we ask ourselves these questions. But when would it have ever been enough? We do the best we can do with what we know at the time. That is all we can do. What I realized as time went on is that I was the one agonizing over the details of all that had happened. Phil was not agonizing over anything. He was literally in Glory Land, and he was content. He was well satisfied. I needed to give myself a break. The last thing Phil would have wanted was for me to be upset in thinking I had not loved on him enough. His main concern for leaving was the people he was leaving behind, how it would hurt them. Why should I, or any of us for that matter, play into the devil's hands, and let the enemy continue to torture us like that? I'm not saying this shift in thinking is easy, or immediate, but it is possible to stop these wrong thoughts with the Holy Spirit's power alive in us.

When I walked to his door, Chris was standing outside it because he had heard the commotion going on. I told him to get Dad.

In the worst of all nightmares, which are our realities, we wonder, is God even watching? Is He even with us? Does He even care? The interesting thing is I had not gone to the door to summon Phil's brother and Dad. I had gone to get Phil some water so he could take some medication. But God was watching, and was there with us, and God was caring more than we could ever know. I had no idea Phil would be leaving us so soon.

Chris, being 20 at the time, said he doesn't know why he didn't go out that night. He thought about it, but stayed home for some reason. Our son, Jimm, had left to go back to his apartment about an hour earlier. He later said that was better for him. But God had Chris standing right outside Phil's door right when I started to leave his room. I didn't ask Chris to go and get some *water,* I told him to go and get his *Dad.* Why? Looking back now, I KNOW it was the Holy Spirit who was in charge of that moment. The Holy Spirit put Chris outside the door, and the Holy Spirit put those words into my mouth, "Go get Dad." Because God knew the time was at hand.

Does that make it all better? All okay? No, it was devastating beyond words. But it was also looked over by a loving God. I can see that so much better looking back. In the moment, things were just happening, without any cognizant planning on my part. As sick as Phil was, even after what had been prayed (I'll talk about that in future chapters), I truly had no idea this was it. When I turned around to go back to his bedside, this is what Phil said:

"Mom, I think God is healing me! I'm really feeling a lot better. I'm going to feel good tomorrow, Mom!"

I said "I love you, Phil," and he said, "I love you."

What if I had left Phil's room and missed that moment with him? What if I had gotten distracted in the kitchen getting his glass of water, only to have returned a short 15 minutes later and found him gone? I hadn't thought about that until just this moment. I would have missed so much, such a tender moment in time to be able to tell him one last time how much I loved him. And to hear him say that he loved me. That's what God provided. God didn't provide an earthly healing, for whatever reason. That only God knows. But God did take care of us while His Kingdom work was proceeding. I don't know, fully, how Phil's dying builds God's Kingdom, but in writing this book, at this present moment, maybe this is all part of it. And Phil did feel better the next day. Just like Phil told me he would.

We all sat around Phil's bed and we talked and shared stories through the tears, and just spent a very special last hour or so with him. Then we prayed and left his room.

I didn't know it then, but these moments in time are etched in a loved-ones' mind for the rest of our days on this earth. These are precious moments that shape our lives. As believers, these moments are guided from the Heavenly realms. We are not thinking clearly, most times. And it will be different for everyone. But whatever it needs to be, it will be. Your "endings" will be very different than ours, but there is no right, and no wrong. We can rest in that. If we had needed something other than what we got, God would have provided it. Whatever we experienced, works for our good when we love God, and "...have been called according to his purpose." (Romans 8:28) It shapes who we are and how we go through future experiences in our life. What we see as so-called "mistakes" on our part, or even if we think they are on God's part, it all helps us do better/different in the future. It is all how we learn and grow. Believers are called the "children" of God for a reason, because we are children here to learn. If we could get it all right, then we would be ready for Heaven ourselves. But we are still here, because God is still molding us and shaping us into all He is calling us to be.

Phil had this smile on his face that I hadn't seen before. Just a little look of "Ahhh, I'm done."

There are special gifts God gives us that are very unexpected. Phil's passing included spastic, almost like electrical misfirings going on with his body. It didn't seem painful, but more like a process of things shutting down. That is why I was surprised to find a smile on his face when I returned to his room. Whatever it is that God will give to us, we should embrace it. The devil's playground is large, and when God enters in, we should run to our Father and hang on tight!

Now if you don't mind, because writing this is very therapeutic for me, I would still like to share this journey with you for a while, maybe for a long while. Maybe this is how I will write my book.

And here we are on this day. If I had not started writing all that I did twelve years ago, I would really have no way of writing this book today. Those thoughts would be long gone. I would only have a vague outline of all that a grieving mom/person goes through in the early, middle, and later stages of grief. I am thankful to be able to look back, and to share it with you today. Thank you for reading my story. I pray it helps you in yours.

Gift #2 – We can start to recognize God's gifts vs. Satan's lies in this world.

What lies has the enemy been trying to fill your head with?

In what ways have you seen God's hand in your circumstances?

Record today's Date and other notes you'd like to make:

The Great

I AM

No, despite all these things, overwhelming victory is ours through Christ who loved us.
Romans 8:37 (NLT)

CHAPTER THREE

"Rabbi," his disciples asked him, "why was this man born blind?
Was it because of his own sins or his parents' sins?"
John 9:2 (NLT)

Me

Good-bye

Sunday, 18 Nov 2001

Tomorrow we bury our son. The child we've cared for, nurtured, disciplined, loved, supported, fed, hugged, taught, and so many endless things we cannot cover them all. The child who trusted us, loved us, teased us, followed us, hugged us, and learned from us. The child God gave to us 16 years ago on October 16, 1985, in Oakland, California.

Philip Andrew Shore came into this world at 2:21 in the afternoon. Recently I asked God to help me let him go, to help me give him back. I needed help to do that. And God reminded me that when Phil was born, the doctor asked Jim if he would like to cut the cord? It took him so by surprise that he declined. So, the doctor asked me if I would like to do it. I said I would, and I did. It was interesting. I remember it like it was yesterday, the thickness of it, and being surprised by that. God reminded me that I cut the cord then, cut Phil away from me, and I must do that again. Release him. God prepared my heart for that when I asked Him to. Ask and you shall receive. I know of no other way that I could have encouraged Phil to go Home; to tell him it was okay to go, that I wanted him to. How could I do that? How could any parent? But I did, with God's strength.

The only thing I asked of Phil in those last days was to please let me be there. I would sit by his bed for hours, and then Jim would come and spend time with him while I took a break. Before I left the room, I would look at Phil very intently, and tell him I was going to get something to eat, or whatever, and please, "Don't leave while I'm gone." God knew how important it was for me to be there at the end, after all we had gone through. I'm a person who likes to finish what I start, and don't get in my way! And I was there, and I'm so grateful to have been.

I was telling people that God answered every prayer we ever prayed, except to heal Philip on this earth. And then this morning it came to me; God answered EVERY prayer we prayed. When Phil said, "Mom, I think God is healing me," He was! God healed Phil on this earth, and then He took him Home. It was his time to go. Phil was finished with what God had called him to do, but not until God, who is ever faithful, answered that last prayer.

When some time had passed, I said, "God, how am I going to go to bed tonight, and get up in the morning with no one to take care of?" It was so difficult to even think about after five and a half years of taking care of Phil. But guess what? God answered that prayer, too. The phone rang first thing that next morning, and I could hear Jim saying, "May I tell her who's calling?" Then he turned to me and said, "Tony missed the bus. He needs a ride to school." Tony is my friend, Linette's, son who lives a few blocks from here. Linette and I met 1½ years ago and have grown very close because she lost her son Gregory at age seven, three years ago. She helps me in so many ways.

I got out of bed, still in my sweats from sleeping with Phil the night before, and sat on the end of my bed to put on my shoes. Bent over tying them, the tears were just dripping as I was smiling and saying to Jim, "God knew I needed someone to take care of this morning." I was seeing God in the details of our lives, and it helped.

Please pray I remember that tomorrow, as we stand beside Phil's coffin on that hill. Please pray I remember that when it is lowered into the grave. Please pray I remember that when we turn and have to walk away and go home. Please pray I remember that when it hurts so bad I can't breathe, and I want to rip my clothing in mourning for him. I could never understand people doing that before when I saw it on TV, or when I heard about that Jewish custom. Now I understand.

*Tomorrow could be the hardest day of our lives. I almost pray that it is, because after that, what would we fear? I don't know how it will be. I don't know if my imaginings could come close. I barely allow my mind to go there. That is tomorrow, and He has given me such a great peace for today. Have I not learned to stay on today? I **have** learned that we won't be alone.*

We are going to play the song that says, "We are standing on Holy ground, and there are angels all around." I know we will feel the presence of God, and He will not leave us to do this alone. He has not brought us this far to abandon us now. I know that. There are many things I know now that I never would have known had it not been for Phil's life, but that doesn't make it easy. It just makes me grateful for my son and all that God taught us through him.

And, I must let him go this one last time, physically. I must walk away and leave him with God.

Please pray... Diane

Myself

Tomorrow we bury our son.

Those are not words I ever thought I'd be writing. Does any parent? And yet so many of us do. They say we are supposed to precede our children in death, but years ago many children preceded their parents in death. There was barely a family that hadn't experienced what today we call so "Wrong." A hundred years ago or more, people had large families to work the farms. They shared the labor, and they shared the grief that came when children died of all sorts of diseases. Today I believe we feel more alone in our grief than parents did then. We wonder...did we do something to cause this? Is God punishing us? Could we have prevented it? I drew comfort from John 9:2-3(NLT): *"Rabbi," his disciples asked him, "Why was this man born blind? Was it because of his own sins or his parents' sins?" "It was not because of his sins or his parents' sins," Jesus answered. "This happened so the power of God could be seen in him."*

The child God gave to us 16 years ago on October 16, 1985, in Oakland, California.

When Phil died, we had choices to make. Do we get angry with God for taking Phil from us, and turn our back on God? Do we blame ourselves? Do we shut down emotionally so we don't ever get this hurt again? Or do we look for God's help with this? We sought God's help. In that, we began to understand that we simply *gave back* to God what He had first given to us. Doing so helped to heal the wound. When we realize that everything we have comes from God, it can help us start to say, "Thank You, Lord, for the sixteen years of joy Phil brought to our lives." What if God had never given him to us in the first place? Oh, what we would have missed out on in knowing and loving such a sweet boy.

God reminded me that I cut the cord then, cut Phil away from me, and I must do that again. Release him.

As the years went by, little by little, I released Phil more and more.

It doesn't happen in the instant our loved one leaves us, but it can happen over time. I remember years later getting to a point where it seemed there was just a thin kite string still attached to Phil. But I was holding on tight. I could feel the tug of that connection, and it would cause my heart to ache. I wanted to let go, but it was so hard. It seemed so disrespectful. It seemed I might forget Phil if I truly let him go. It seemed I must hang onto something to keep him with me, and to keep my love for him alive. What I have found since cutting that last kite string and letting Phil go completely, is that now I get to keep all of him in my healed heart. The parts that I would not let go of were the parts that would not heal in God's way. The memories of our loved ones are actually more fully enjoyed when we really begin to trust God to keep them in His loving care until we see them again.

"God, how am I going to go to bed tonight, and get up in the morning with no one to take care of?"

As I drove Tony to school that next morning, I was so thankful to have a reason to get out of bed. I told Tony that Phil was with his brother, Gregory, now. Surprised, he asked, "He died?" I said, "Yes, last night." We rode the rest of the way in silence. I will never forget the gift God gave me that morning, the gift of being able to get out of bed with a purpose. And I would imagine Tony will never forget that morning either. Moments, frozen in time, help us grow closer to one another and to our God.

Tomorrow could be the hardest day of our lives.

I heard a woman in her mid 70's speak at a conference a couple of years after we buried our son. She talked of her son who was in Heaven, and that it was his birthday. I went up to her after she finished speaking to ask her a question. I just had to ask her if losing her son was the hardest thing she had ever had to do in her life? After all, I was only in my early 40's. Maybe it even gets worse than this? She told me that it *was* the hardest thing she had ever done. I was relieved to hear it. With her answer, I knew that God was bringing us through one of the worst things that could happen in life, and it helped me to know that with God all things truly *are* possible, even the hardest things. Slowly but surely, I was learning.

And, I must let him go this one last time, physically. I must walk away and leave him with God.

When we left the cemetery that day, we truly did feel God's presence with us. It was a quiet ride home in the car. It was unbelievable that we could watch Phil's coffin being lowered into the ground and have any sense of sanity left. I truly believe God places a protective fog around those who grieve in the early days, because if the full reality set in immediately, it would be more than our mind could endure. Little by little it settles in—and little by little God brings us through. But there does come a point when we hit the bottom, which I will tell you about in future chapters.

Please Pray...

We had so many people praying for us. It really did help to share our lives with those around us, because then they could continue to pray for us through the years. It's hard to share such pain with others. It's hard to be with other people. We want to hide away. People say things that can hurt us. Or they ignore us because of their discomfort. It's really up to us to help them feel comfortable around grief. I know it seems unfair that we should need to reach out when we are the ones so broken. But if they don't learn from us, who will they learn from? People don't mean to harm us, they just have never been taught how gently we need to be handled.

<u>Gift #3</u> – God's protective fog helps get us through those early days.

Have you had a sense of God's protection, however slight, in your own sorrow?

Are you sharing your heart with others so they are able to pray for you? Why or why not?

Record today's date and other notes you'd like to make:

The Great

<u>I AM</u>

"It was not because of his sins or his parents' sins," Jesus answered. "This happened so the power of God could be seen in him."
John 9:3 (NLT)

CHAPTER FOUR

And now, dear brothers and sisters, we want you to know
what will happen to the believers who have died, so you
will not grieve like people who have no hope.
1 Thessalonians 4:13 (NLT)

<u>Me</u>

As the Day Draws to a Close

Monday, 19 Nov 2001

Where do I start to tell you about this day? This very important, all
absorbing day? As it draws to a close, I need to tell you, though. I
need to tell you because I know so many of you have prayed for us
today. Many of you are concerned, and others wish you could have
been with us to say good-bye to Phil, however difficult that would
have been. But may I tell you, thank you. Thank you for allowing
us to keep this private, to keep it simple, and to let us bury Phil in
the way of our choosing. We are grateful to you for letting us do
things a bit different than some, and for supporting us even if you
didn't understand. Part of us wishes you had been there, because it
was very special to us. But the other part is very grateful to be

able to say good-bye to him in this way. He was a quiet boy with a great sense of humor, and doing this quietly seemed appropriate.

So many on this day would spend the time after the burial shaking hands, giving hugs, sharing food and stories of their loved one. We didn't. We came home, got comfortable, put in the movie "Heaven Can Wait," (Strange, you may think?) and I curled up with a blanket. It felt so good. It felt so good to reflect on what had just happened...to soak it all in and to run it all through my mind again and again: how we arrived at the cemetery, walked to the casket and stood looking at it, light blue, not so large, five chairs lined up next to it, cloudy sky, but pretty. The sky was light blue, with hints of sunshine breaking through. We stood for a short time, and then we listened to, "We are Standing on Holy Ground." It was beautiful, and the tears rolled easily. It felt like Holy ground. Jim prayed and spoke of God's presence being where two or more are gathered. God was there; we felt Him. I saw Him in the skies; I breathed Him in. He gave us peace. I looked at Phil's picture beside the casket, and remembered his sweet face. It smiled back at me. Jim read 1 Thessalonians 4:13-18 and 5:1-11 and then we played a song, "Good-bye for Now." How comforting to know it is just for now.

Then Jim started to read this:

Philip Andrew Shore
October 16, 1985 - November 14, 2001

*Our son, our brother...we are here, but you are not. Although it seems to us, in our human thinking, that you are contained in this box. What **is** here is not you, but merely the tent you inhabited while you walked on this earth with us—the tent that housed you, the tent that grew with you, the tent that we all saw with our eyes, and that we recognized you by.*

The morning sun has risen now. The tent's flap has been opened and you have walked out into the light that shines from God; into His warmth and His love. You heard His call to come Home and that is where you are now. This tent leaked human tears. It blew in earthly storms. It blocked the clear view of Heaven and was staked down unable to fly, and it has been left behind. You are free!

Your eyes now see a new world that is beyond our imagination, while we are still here in our tents. Your pain has ended; ours will linger. Your eyes will not cry another tear, while many will fall from ours. Your body will no longer suffer. How happy we are for you!

We are happy for your freedom—happy to know that you fought the good fight and have now been released from your earthly bondage to start your time of Heavenly eternity with God, and our Savior Jesus Christ.

Christ knew what it was like to walk in this flesh, to hurt in this flesh, and He welcomes you Home with open arms. We're sure He's saying, "Well done, my good and faithful servant." You were faithful, grown beyond your years in many ways, and yet still a child at heart—just the combination that Jesus is happy to see, trusting Him with a childlike faith.

To say we will not miss you would be the ultimate lie, but to say that we know where you are and that you are happy and so loved is the ultimate Truth. We are secure in that, and all God has promised us. We cry on this day, and we also rejoice at your Homecoming. You are free; so free. You suffer no more!

You have taught us so much, and we will remember you all our days. Hopefully, as the days go by, there will be more laughter than tears, until the day comes when we will leave our tents and walk out into God's beautiful and all comforting light of Heaven.

As we leave here today, it's with heavy hearts. But blessed are those who mourn, for we will feel the comfort that God is giving and continue to grow closer to Him until we see you again.

We are happy for you, Phil. Your time was short in our eyes, but the memory of how you touched our lives will be everlasting.

"To live is Christ and to die is gain."

Your gentle, loving spirit was evidence of Christ living in you, and now you have gained all that He promised you when He paved the way to Heaven for all believers.

We love you Phil.

We miss you.

Welcome Home!

God gave me a poem this morning called Heaven's Door. I didn't know if I would be able to read it or not, but I took it, and thanks to the peace of God and His strength, I was able to read it. It goes:

Heaven's Door

Today we bury you, my son, we put you in the ground
Turn and walk away from you, leave you behind until the sound
Of trumpets fill the air, the sky, and Jesus Christ we see
Gathering all His children, to spend eternity
Together with our Risen Lord, the One who made us whole
The One who has redeemed us, from Satan and his pull
Of death and graves and misery, of lies and plain deceit
Yes, Jesus Christ is Risen, and we'll all bow at His feet
Worship Him and praise Him, even more so than before
Thank Him for the gift of life, and for opening the door
To Heaven and the promise, that we will be with Him
Together with other believers, cleansed from our earthly sin
We place you in the ground today, but you're not really here
It's just another lie from Satan, to bring on another tear
You live my son, you're living, more than you ever have before
Free from pain and suffering, you passed through Heaven's door

Sons, Jimm, and Chris had gone out and bought five blue roses (I know. I didn't know they existed either.) and they had a green ribbon tied around each one. I handed a blue rose to everyone, and then I walked over and picked up some dirt, walked to the grave and sprinkled it in and then tossed in my blue rose.

Our Pastor, Dave, then read a wonderful Psalm, 127.

Unless the Lord builds the house, its builders labor in vain.
Unless the Lord watches over the city,
the watchmen stand guard in vain.
In vain you rise early and stay up late,
toiling for food to eat – for he grants sleep to those he loves.
Sons are a heritage from the Lord, children a reward from him.
Like arrows in the hands of a warrior,
are sons born in one's youth.
Blessed is the man whose quiver is full of them.
They will not be put to shame when they contend with
their enemies in the gate.
Psalm 127(NIV)

We gathered in a tight circle and Dave prayed. I don't remember all that he prayed, but I remember that when he prayed for me, it spoke to my heart, as I'm sure it did when he prayed for each one of us. I don't remember the exact words, but the general idea to me was; this has been a great loss, but Jim, Jimm, and Chris are still here with me, and I need to remember that. I need to love them and cherish them, just as I have Phil. (Sorry for the interpretation Dave, I know these were not the words, but I know that this is what God put in your heart to pray for me to hear. It is exactly what I needed to hear.)

Then we played the song, "God is in Control." "...He's watching over you and me." When it got to that part, I looked up at Jim and we smiled at each other, knowing how true this was. My parents had given us two red roses, a heart shaped balloon, and a balloon that said, "God Bless You." We put those at the graveside, and then we left.

We rode the 15 minutes home in almost complete silence and awe I think. I know I was experiencing that peace that transcends understanding. All I kept noticing was how beautiful the sky looked with the wispy white clouds and baby blue background. It hadn't rained on us, and now it could pour if it wanted to. I was headed home to curl up in a blanket, which is exactly what I did. It's hard to explain to you how I felt, but I told Jim that I wondered if this is what Valium felt like? He said, "This is even better than Valium." I believe he is right. How anyone can feel such peace on a day such as this, is beyond human understanding. To be able to just stay quiet and reflect on that very special hour by the graveside was a gift. I've heard it's the day after that is so hard because everyone goes home, and there is such silence. I relished this silence. The love of God filled every part of my being.

The tears will still fall, and we will forever miss Phil. But the hardest day of our life was blessed by our good and loving God, who never leaves us and never forsakes us. He carries us through the storms and wraps us in His loving arms.

Good night everyone and thank you for all the prayers today. They were felt ten-fold.
Please know that!

The Shore Family

Myself

Thank you for allowing us to keep this private, to keep it simple, and to let us bury Phil in the way of our choosing. We are grateful to you for letting us do things a bit different than some, and for supporting us even if you didn't understand.

Looking back 12 years later, I'm not sure we did what was right, but at the time we did what we thought best, and that is all any of us can ask of ourselves. Sure, there were things we missed and probably people that we hurt along the way. But everyone, and I MEAN EVERYONE, needs to be more understanding through these times because emotions are running wild, and decisions are not always made in the best interest of everyone. There is not a lot of time to make decisions. Normally, there's only three days until burial. We had five. Really? I think one of the smartest things we did was wait at least two weeks before Phil's celebration service. And even that seemed fast to put together a lifetime of memories to share with those who would be at his service. God surely helped us do it. Looking back, we saw that clearly.

...to soak it all in, and to run it all through my mind again and again; how we arrived at the cemetery, walked to the casket and stood looking at it.

These moments really do soak into your soul: the sounds, the tears, the touches. I remember Chris holding my hand as I sat before his brother's coffin. I remember the boys being so strong, so sweet, so broken too… I remember getting up and picking up some dirt that had been piled there and tossing it into Phil's grave, hearing it strike against what contained the child I love so dearly. It was abrasive and disturbing. Then I tossed in the blue rose the boys had picked up earlier to bring with us. These memories do not fade; they sit within us forever, and they NEED the Hope we have in Jesus to be lived through. Getting stuck in those moments can destroy us, but they don't have to.

We are here, but you are not. Although it seems to us, in our human thinking that you are contained in this box.

I had a grieving Mom once ask me, "Are they cold?" It was winter, and our children both lay buried in the ground. I reassured her, they are not cold. They are in Heaven. They are being well taken care of. It was a question she needed to ask of a Mom who would understand where our thoughts can go.

Your body will no longer suffer. How happy we are for you!

If you ever wonder about unconditional love, I believe this is how we can show it—not to those on earth with us, but to those who have gone to Heaven before us. We can be happy for them. Their suffering is over. Would we really want to keep them here, just so that *we* can feel better? That is why I would want Phil here today. But that would be selfish of me. Phil paid his dues. He fought the good fight, and I want him to be at peace now, no matter how hard that is for me. We have to love them that much.

To say we will not miss you would be the ultimate lie, but to say that we know where you are and that you are happy and so loved is the ultimate Truth. We are secure in that, and all God has promised us.

God allowed me to write these words. He helped me write them. He wanted me to believe them with all my heart. But that took time. We can voice many things; we can even walk it out. But to truly believe it, deep in our souls, takes a lot of practice. God understands that. God just wants us to work with Him on it until His healing shows it to be true for ourselves. When it becomes true to us, then we can truly comfort another with the comfort we have been given. As spoken in 2 Corinthians 1:4 (NLT), "He comforts us in all our troubles so that we can comfort others."

Hopefully as the days go by, there will be more laughter than tears.

My sister wondered if I would ever smile again, let alone laugh. Grief is worn, visibly on and through our bodies. Those around us can feel it. It causes them discomfort. They don't know what to do to "make" us happy. Oh, they want to. They would do anything to take away our pain. But it stays with us, until God has worked it through and out of us in His own way, and in His own time. We MUST cooperate with God, even though everything in us fights against it. I will share more of that in future chapters—the things God asked me to do when I surely didn't want to. All this to say, I smile and laugh a lot twelve years later. There truly is great joy in the "morning."

...the memory of how you touched our lives will be everlasting.

We really are afraid if we let go, we will forget. Don't worry. We don't forget. EVER! Whatever impact our loved ones had on our life will stay with us. We will run through our thoughts about them more times than we will ever be able to count, and slowly but surely we will start to weed out the ones that cause us pain, if we are wise, and hold close the ones that warm our hearts. This, too, takes practice. We want to think of all the things we could have done better. Believe me, our loved ones NO LONGER CARE about the mistakes we may have made. The only thing they are thinking is how much God loves them, and how good Heaven is compared to earth. They aren't even missing us right now, although they will be there to greet us when we arrive, and yes, give us a big welcoming hug. We will have bodies in Heaven, and we will recognize each other.

Turn and walk away from you, leave you behind until the sound
Of trumpets fill the air, the sky, and Jesus Christ we see.

If you've never thought much about Jesus' return, you might start thinking of it more while grieving. I sure did, and do. We are all getting out of here, and some of us will even get out of here alive! When Jesus comes back, reunions will be taking place. I now end my prayers with the last part of Revelation, "Amen. Come, Lord, Jesus!" And when I have the privilege of being with those who are leaving this earth behind, I ask them to please ask Jesus to come back **soon** when they see Him. What a great Hope we have in Jesus!

Jim, Jimm, and Chris are still here with me, and I need to
remember that. I need to love them and cherish them, just as I
have Phil.

This may make perfect sense, but it is very hard. I say this in all honesty, but with reservation, because it doesn't "sound good." But, loving those God has left you with, and not wanting to just die with the one God has taken, is difficult. There is so much pain in your heart; it takes everything inside to just keep on breathing. Being able to give love to others becomes almost impossible. I knew my husband and my other sons needed me. Jim still needed a wife, Jimm and Chris still needed a Mom. But miraculously, God cared for them when I could not. Eighty five percent of marriages will end due to the death of a child. Everyone, once again, EVERYONE, needs to be more than understanding toward each other during these extremely difficult times. Otherwise, the enemy will tear a marriage and a family apart. Satan is out to kill, steal and destroy, and he's very good at it. With time, and the healing power of Jesus, Satan can be defeated. Our family is living proof of that. Yours can be too. To God be the Glory!

How can anyone feel such peace on a day such as this, is beyond human understanding. To be able to just stay quiet and reflect on that very special hour by the grave side was a gift.

These gifts of peace come from God. There is no other way to explain them. They certainly don't come from us. They certainly don't come from our enemy, Satan. They come straight from Heaven, through the Holy Spirit, and into our hearts, to help us. And these times of peace are so necessary along the way. Without a break in the "storm," we would go under for sure. These gifts of peace became a part of my daily routine. They can become a part of yours. How? Be pro-active in the healing process. Spend time with God. It's a MUST! I would go to my room for up to two hours at a time, and draw close to God. I'd cry, pray, read His Word, pray again, cry some more, ask for help, help, help! I called this time my, "God Pill," and I needed it often in the beginning to ease the pain. I might have survived physically without spending this time with God, but I never could have thrived emotionally and spiritually without it. God is there for all who will seek His face. He promises us that, and God doesn't lie. Jesus will help us through the power of the Holy Spirit that lives within.

Gift #4 – Discovering the peace Jesus left us with...a peace that surpasses all understanding.

Have you ever experienced peace when it almost seemed inappropriate?

What Bible verse brings you comfort? If you don't have one, try reading Psalm 91.

Record today's date and other notes you'd like to make:

The Great

I AM

For since we believe that Jesus died and was raised to life again, we also believe that when Jesus returns, God will bring back with him the believers who have died.
1 Thessalonians 4:14 (NLT)

CHAPTER FIVE

"Do not let your hearts be troubled. Trust in God, trust also in me. In my Father's house are many rooms, if it were not so, I would have told you. I am going there to prepare a place for you. And if I go and prepare a place for you, I will come back and take you to be with me that you also may be where I am. You know the way to the place where I am going."

Thomas said to him, "Lord, we don't know where you are going, so how can we know the way?"

Jesus answered, "I am the way and the truth and the life. No one comes to the Father except through me. If you really knew me, you would know my Father as well. From now on, you do know him and have seen him."

Philip said, "Lord, show us the Father and that will be enough for us."

Jesus answered: "Don't you know me, Philip, even after I have been among you such a long time?"

"Anyone who has seen me has seen the Father. How can you say, 'Show us the Father'? Don't you believe that I am in the Father and that the Father is in me? The words I say to you are not just my own. Rather, it is the Father, living in me, who is doing his work."

John 14:1-10 (NLT)

Me

Thanksgiving

Thursday, 22 Nov 2001

*"...it is the Father, living in me, who is doing his work." How would I live each day without that? I mean, I could get up and try to breathe, and go through the motions of what looked like living. But what about **really** living? What about real Thanksgiving... especially today? Today is the day Phil LOVED! He was a turkey boy—turkey and dressing. One year he even had it for his birthday. He didn't care if it was Stove Top, or out of the turkey on Thanksgiving. He just had to have it, and often.*

I wonder, why didn't he hang on until at least Thanksgiving? You know, as some people do? They make it through the Holidays, and then go Home? But he didn't. I thought maybe it was because he wasn't eating anyway. And then Jim said to me yesterday, "He wanted Heaven more than he wanted turkey." Boy, that's for sure! Once he caught a glimpse of Heaven, he longed for it. How can I blame him? I long for it, and I haven't even seen it.

*Yesterday, the verse, "Do not let your hearts be troubled," kept running through my mind. We had a busy day yesterday. We were finishing up Obituary papers, ordering Phil's grave marker, and a number of other things. And that verse was with me **all** day. I thought of Thanksgiving, and everyone who would be celebrating today. And I know many of you will be thinking about us today.*

How will we make it through? To tell you the truth, I really don't know how we will do. It's still morning, and I haven't gotten a "whiff" of turkey cooking yet. That will be at my sister's house here in Pleasanton later. But, I have a feeling that the thinking will be harder than the doing of it. When we do it, God carries us. When we think about it, we drown in our own sorrows. That's not what God intended. The Word says:

Rejoice in the Lord always. I will say it again: Rejoice! Let your gentleness be evident to all. The Lord is near. Do not be anxious about anything, but in everything, by prayer and petition, with THANKSGIVING, present your requests to God. And the peace of God, which transcends all understanding, will guard your hearts and your minds in Christ Jesus.

Finally, brothers, whatever is true, whatever is noble, whatever is right, whatever is pure, whatever is lovely, whatever is admirable – if anything is excellent or praiseworthy – think about such things. Philippians 4:4-8 (NIV)

*"Think about such things." I think about that line. Should I be thinking about all the sad things that can cause tears to fall? Or should I be thinking about all the good things, all the praiseworthy things, all the right things? I think I should. Does it honor Phil to drum up misery? No! I told him we would be fine. I assured him of that. I told him we would miss him, but when I thought about missing him I would think about how good **he** feels, and I would be happy for him. That's what I told him. If I don't do that, if I drown in my sorrow, I have lied to my son. That would dishonor him, and he would not be happy to know that. Do I have a hole the size of the Grand Canyon in my gut? **Yes**...I do! Does my heart ache? **Yes**...it does! But am I thankful? **Yes**, I am...so **very** thankful! I'm thankful for the Hope we have. I am thankful for our wonderful sons. I am thankful for this day, that we can rejoice in the Lord and all His promises. Will I shed tears today? I imagine I will. But I hope they are a mixture of joy, and sadness, and missing, and Hope. I think they will be. Those we will be gathering with also*

miss Philip. They will understand the tears. They will also understand the Hope we have in Jesus.

*Jim says it's like in the olden days when the Europeans set out across the ocean for the new land. When they said good-bye, they knew they would probably never see their family again. Maybe there would be an occasional letter, but it was doubtful. The only thing they knew was that they were going to start a new life, in a new land, and that was a good thing. They didn't even know if they would be okay when they got there. Well, Phil has done the same. He has gone to a new life, in a new "land." But we DO KNOW that he is okay. He's **more** than okay! That helps me breathe, and that helps me get through each day without him until I see him again.*

A friend told me that she had a dream about Phil, and he was out in a beautiful, colorful field playing ball. He said, "I'm playing ball because I wasn't able to do that on earth." I have run that picture through my mind many, many times. It's the little things like that, that help a lot.

Today we will guard our hearts and our minds in Christ Jesus. We will feel the peace which transcends all understanding. And we will give Thanks for God's abundance in our lives, and the Hope of one day living in the Father's House where Christ has gone to prepare a place for us.

HAPPY THANKSGIVING TO YOU ALL! Rejoice! Again I say, rejoice!

Love, The Shore Family

<u>Myself</u>

*"...it is the Father living in me, who is doing his work." How would I live each day without that? I mean, I could get up and try to breathe, and go through the motions of what looked like living. But what about **really** living? What about real Thanksgiving...*

especially today?

The Holidays; all were difficult, for a long time...always emotionally charged. But impossible to get through? No. They are very possible to get through with God. Just this last Christmas, our 12th without our son, Phil, we took our annual Christmas Eve picture. There were 12 of us in that family picture; God has added two daughters-in-law to our family, and six grandchildren. When we compare that with the picture taken just a month after I wrote this about Thanksgiving, where there were only four of us in the picture, it is picture proof that life can still be amazingly wonderful. My friend, Michella, said, when looking at the picture of the four of us that first Christmas, "That is messed up." I had to agree, but I also have to say that it has gone from messed up, to blessed up.

I wonder, why didn't he hang on until at least Thanksgiving? You know, as some people do?

Everyone will have a particular holiday, maybe more than one, that is especially painful. Knowing that the person we are missing loved the festivities of that special day can make us not want to celebrate it at all. That is perfectly understandable. The second Thanksgiving that Phil was gone, I didn't want to do Thanksgiving. I just wanted it to be over. An interesting thing was said to me on that day. I was told that, "It wouldn't get better" as the years went on. Everything inside of me fought against that thought. It actually spurred me on to prove that statement wrong. I wanted God's Word to be true. I wanted God's Word to be healing. And I wanted to challenge God to do what He says He will do in His Word. If He didn't, I would gladly tell the world that it doesn't work. But, I'm here 12 years later to tell the world that it does work! And it does get better with Jesus as our Eternal Hope.

Once he caught a glimpse of Heaven, he longed for it. How can I blame him? I long for it, and I haven't even seen it.

Phil shared an experience with me shortly before he went Home. I like to say Phil, "Went Home," instead of "Phil died," because Phil is alive. His body died; that is for sure. But his spirit is fully alive in his new Home in Heaven. And shortly before he left, he got a glimpse of Heaven. I don't know how this happens, but I do know that my son was not a story-teller; he spoke the truth. And to be with your loved-one when they say they have seen Heaven, and that it is so beautiful, and that they want to be there. That's a miraculous moment in life! This is one I have never forgotten, and one that has helped me through many a dark time in my personal grief walk. The Holidays on this earth, the celebrations we have, are NOTHING compared to the **Celebration** that takes place in Heaven every single day.

How will we make it through? To tell you the truth, I really don't know how we will do.

We did make it through that first Thanksgiving, and many more to follow. They were difficult, and emotional. But God will never leave us. He will give us the strength we need, when we need it. Sometimes it seems God gives us just enough strength, and sometimes it seems He gives us more than enough. But either way, as the years go on, so will we with God's help. It seems some days ahead can loom so large, like huge mountains with no way around them. God takes us *through* each mountain, one step at a time… helping us dig through the rubble of our lives. Even when the steps are weary, they are still steps. Time and God will heal what is so broken. Time alone will not do it. Time needs to be used wisely *with* God each step of the way.

Should I be thinking about all the sad things that can cause tears to fall, or should I be thinking about all the good things, all the praiseworthy things, all the right things.

Our minds are powerful tools. They can be used to build us up, or they can be used to destroy us. In the beginning, it seems we have little choice where our minds go in our grief. We have not yet learned how to stop the thoughts that torture us. Maybe there is a good reason for that. Maybe it's like cleaning house and figuring out what we need to keep, and what we need to get rid of. But if we are wise, we will start to discard the thoughts that make our heart ache. If we are wise, we will start to see them coming along our path, the disastrous detours that loom ahead, and we will choose not to turn toward those distractions, but instead keep our minds on *whatever is true, whatever is noble, whatever is right, whatever is pure, whatever is lovely, whatever is admirable – if anything is excellent or praiseworthy – think about such things.* Philippians 4:4-8 (NIV)

*Does it honor Phil to drum up misery? No! I told him we would be fine. I assured him of that. I told him we would miss him, but when I thought about missing him I would think about how good **he** feels, and I would be happy for him.*

I really can't talk about our thought patterns enough here. Staying focused is so important! It is good to work through all our thoughts. It is good to talk them out with God, first and foremost, and then with those we can trust. Writing our thoughts down is great therapy. But our thoughts should be worked *through*, so they don't become like quicksand–where we get stuck and then pulled under. Our loved ones would not want us to be miserable. It's hard to believe it's right to feel good again someday. But it is. People have been dying since the beginning of time. Everyone in this world will eventually say good-bye to someone they care deeply about. And God is the same God throughout all time. Our Father in Heaven does not want His children to quit living life because of death. He wants us to know that Jesus conquered death for all time by rising from His own grave, and providing eternal life for all who will believe in Him. *...so you will not be full of sorrow like people who have no hope. For since we believe that Jesus died and was raised to life again, we also believe that when Jesus comes, God will bring back with Jesus all the Christians who have died. 1 Thessalonians 4:13&14 (NLT)*

*Do I have a hole the size of the Grand Canyon in my gut? **Yes**...I do! Does my heart ache? **Yes**...it does! But am I thankful? **Yes**, I am.*

Grief cuts into the very deepest part of our soul. The soul is our mind, our will, and our emotions. Grief touches all three. It makes a huge impact in our lives. We probably know those who have never recovered. They don't mean to harm those around them by staying sad forever. They truly believe they are doing what is right. They believe that by staying sad, it is the best way to honor those they are missing. It feels right to feel bad. But God can fill that huge hole inside of us, eventually. Not overnight, not in a year, but eventually when we walk it out with Him, He will bring us through. Being healed from our pain is what our Father wants for us. God wants His Holy Spirit within us to grow to the point that the huge hole in us is filled with His abundant love. And then, that His love becomes so large in us, it overflows onto others who need to know about the Hope we have in Jesus. On the contrary, the enemy wants to bury us alive. Satan wants to make the hole even bigger than it is. But however big the hole is, God will help us rebuild our lives by pouring His strong foundation in that hole. By using prayer, His Word, His body of believers, and anything else that He provides, we can live again. We need all these things. We need to put them to full use. When we see the rebuilding start to happen, we can be happy about it! When we start to live in the Hope of Jesus' Resurrection, understanding that He truly conquered death, we can begin to understand the true meaning of Thanksgiving deep in our heart.

Will I shed tears today? I imagine I will. But I hope they are a mixture of joy, and sadness, and missing, and Hope.

Tears are good. They wash our hearts clean. They are a natural part of grief, and they will last for many years, probably for the rest of our lives. But, they will diminish over time. In the beginning, they come quickly and frequently. Later on down the road, they won't be as guttural. Tears of grief have a nature all their own. If you have cried them, you know what I'm talking about. You recognize them from other tears. When Phil was just born, I had a night of "grief tears." I didn't know what they were at the time. But he wasn't more than a week old or so, and I couldn't stop the tears, all night long. They came in waves, and they came from deep inside of me. I wonder now, all these years later, if somewhere in my spirit I knew that I would not be keeping this child of mine. I didn't experience that with our other two boys. I had some postpartum sadness, but nothing like that one night of "grief tears" when Phil was a newborn.

He has gone to a new life, in a new "land." But we DO KNOW that he is okay!

This has to be a **must**! We have to know that our loved ones are still living, and know that they are okay. We have to know that God has them in His care, and we need not worry about them. We have enough to think about down here, just taking care of ourselves. Of course, sometimes, we wonder about their eternity. Some people are not vocal about their belief in Jesus Christ. Some are, and have told us they are not interested in Christ as their Savior. But only our Father in Heaven knows a person's last thoughts on this earth. I knew of a man who almost died on the battlefield in Vietnam. He made it out alive, to tell us the story. He said if he had died in the war, no one in his family would have known about his faith. He had never told them. They might have grieved, not only his death, but his eternal life, thinking he was in Hell. It would not have been true. If your loved one is gone, and you aren't sure where they are living out their eternity, trust God with their souls. Trust God that He has their best interest at heart. Trust God that He has given them every opportunity to say yes to Jesus before their final departure from this earth. Our Father wants that none should be lost, and we can rest in His plan for their eternal lives.

"I'm playing ball because I wasn't able to do that on earth." I have run that picture through my mind many, many times. It's the little things like that, that help a lot.

A word can come through anyone. I did not know this woman well, but she had a word for me that my heart needed to hear. A hopeful picture of Phil, well, and happy, and able to do what his earthly body would not let him do. These are gifts that God gives to those who grieve. There will be many along the way. Watch for them. Embrace them. Let them be just what they are, a little salve on an open wound, clearing out infection and allowing for healing.

Today we will guard our hearts and our minds in Christ Jesus.

In Christ Jesus is the only place we can truly live again, because **He** lives. Death is SO final. It can make us crazy. It seems so impossible that the person we were just with is no longer with us. Without the strong fortress that comes in knowing Christ and the Hope of His Resurrection, we have no solid ground on which to stand. Everything in our world has been shaken to the core. Only Christ stands firm, unmoving, always the same, always hopeful, always confident, always sure. We have to stand behind His shield of faith, holding onto His Truth, or our hearts and our minds will not survive such a vicious attack of grief on our souls. We **need** the One who is in us, *because the one who is in you is greater than the one who is in the world. 1 John 4:4(NIV)* The Enemy wants us to think he is all so powerful. And Satan does yield a lot of power, but it's nothing close to what our Savior's power can do with a soul that is devoted to Him!

Gift #5 – Learning to live in the power of the Holy Spirit that is available to all who believe!

What seemingly impossible situation has God brought you through?

Does that experience, and Christ in you, give you confidence in facing the future?

Record today's date and other notes you'd like to make:

The Great

<u>I AM</u>

We can rejoice, too, when we run into problems and trials, for we know that they help us develop endurance. And endurance develops strength of character, and character strengthens our confident hope of salvation. And this hope will not lead to disappointment. For we know how dearly God loves us, because he has given us the Holy Spirit to fill our hearts with his love.
Romans 5:3-5 (NLT)

CHAPTER SIX

We love because he first loved us.
1 John 4:19 (NIV)

Me

Each Day

Sunday, 25 Nov 2001

"Because He lives, I can face tomorrow."

Jim and I were just listening to that song on a video, and it so spoke to my heart. Because He lives, I CAN face tomorrow. Otherwise, what would tomorrow hold for me? Just heartache and tears, and just missing and sorrow? That's not tomorrow. That's depression and misery. I don't want to live like that—not with all the gifts that are left to enjoy until my time has come to join Phil. Yes, sometimes I wish it were soon, and yet I know it could be 40 plus years. It's just the crazy thinking of a mother; a mother who misses her child greatly. A mother who looks at his sweet picture, and longs for the face I see. A mother who runs the events over and over in her mind until it becomes a heavy burden that needs to be unloaded. And I unload it. I tell it to God, I tell it to Jim, and I write until my heart has nothing left to write. I cry. But I'm not a big crier, so it is only part of my grieving process. I imagine all people grieve differently. I tend to feel the tears more at night, as I grow tired and my defenses are depleted. That's when my "nourishment" for the day is running low. I think watching that video of worship music tonight will keep me fed until the day is done now.

I'm sleeping okay. But when I wake up, no matter what time it is, I'm usually done sleeping. My mind starts to "think," and the reality comes back. Nothing a good cup of coffee, a cozy blanket, and the Psalms can't calm though. To read of God's great power, and His love for us, could calm any spirit; even in the most trying of times.

Jim and I were just talking about this being the worst thing we will probably ever face, and it's not so bad. How can we say that? Because, there are times when we feel okay, and even times when we feel good. The times when our hearts ache the most don't last too long—just long enough to teach us that we need God, and He is our only source of peace. The minute I think my peace is found **anywhere else**, I quickly learn it is **not**. The minute I puff myself up and think, "Wow, I'm doing okay here," it soon passes. We need to grieve, and we need to miss. We need to **know** all these emotions, or we will never heal. We could bury them under busyness and a forced smile (as the "world" sometimes tells us to). But then I don't believe we would fully heal.

I ask God to please help me to feel all that I need to feel to heal correctly. I don't want to get a few years down the road and find out that I've made little progress. One of my mottoes is like the Nike ad, "Just do it"! I just want to do it, and I don't want to waste time in the process. Yes, it's a strange personality I have, but God knows what He's doing.

.......Thank you Faith! That's a friend who just called to encourage me. To say keep writing. Keep revealing. And not only will I heal, *but others will heal. God knew I needed that word of encouragement right at that moment. I was doubtful if this e-mail would be sent. I was doubtful if I should be so open about my inner turmoil and grieving process. I don't know how I'm supposed to grieve. I don't know what is correct, or what is even disrespectful. Will people think I didn't love my son if I smile? If I wasn't SURE of my love for him, I probably would not be able to smile. The pressure from what the world says is so contradictory from what God says, and God's way is the healthy way. I have to believe that, because it is the only thing that brought Phil comfort in his final hours. And it is the only thing that brings me comfort now.*

"For my thoughts are not your thoughts, neither are your ways my ways," declares the Lord. "As the heavens are higher than the earth, so are my ways higher than your ways and my thoughts than your thoughts." Isaiah 55:8-9 (NIV)

God's Word is anointed. I told Phil that. Even if he didn't understand what I was reading, just hearing it would help. It did. And even if now my mind wanders while I read, just reading soothes my soul.

This week we will be making final preparations for Phil's service on Saturday. I know we will have lots of helping hands, and they are much appreciated. Phil didn't know any of these plans, except that Dave would be doing his service. We did discuss if that would be okay with him. The rest is just coming together, as the days pass by. When everything is done prayerfully, the stress is minimal. We can be assured that what happens will be in God's plan.

God's plan...it's so different from ours, but so perfect. To know that God is in control of my broken heart is the only way that it will heal correctly. It may take five years, or the rest of my life, but little by little I will grow stronger as He grows in me. When I empty my burdens on Him and allow Him to carry them, I breathe easier. That's all I need right now, to be able to breathe. The rest

we will work on one day at a time.
Love, Diane

You Love Me

How can I face another day Lord, without my precious boy
I can because You love me, and with You I can feel joy
How can I face another night Lord, without his face to kiss
I can because You love me, and You know how he is missed
How can I face another person, and tell them You are good
I can because You love me, and because of where I've stood
I've stood with You Lord, beside his open grave
Given up my child Lord, back to You on that day
And I felt uplifted, beyond even my grief
Because You love me, I was able to see
In death the only victory, is won by You
Because You conquered it, You pulled us through
Through the fiery grip, that kept us bound
And You set our feet, on solid ground
With Your foundation, we need not shake
And tremble fearfully, for it only takes
Your Word and Your love, to rescue us
Help me Lord Jesus, to always trust
In all You've promised, from this day forth
I need You more now, than ever before
And what I'm needing, cannot be found
Here on this earth, there's nothing around
That can ever satisfy, this ache in me
Just You my Savior, and Your promise of eternity

Myself

Because He lives, I CAN face tomorrow.

I really didn't know if I could, but I sure hoped I could. I hung on like I really might be able to get through Phil's Homegoing. It seemed "iffy." But what choice did I have? To go and join him was not a choice that would benefit anyone, including me. I had to stick around and do the best I could. The only thing is, the best I could wasn't enough. I needed the best that God could do for me. On my own, I was a totally desperate soul, and I knew it. I was in waaaaay over my head with this one! One friend asked me, shortly before Phil's Homegoing, how I was doing? I said, "Without God, I can't even walk. With God, I can run." We are called to run this race. God never said it would be easy, or without sweat and tears. But God said He would always be with us. He has been with me, just as He will be with you. You might not notice Him until you take a look back, but then you *will* see He was there all along.

...a mother who misses her child greatly. A mother who looks at his sweet picture, and longs for the face I see.

Pictures are so precious, yet so difficult, in the beginning. There they are, the ones we love, right there in a photograph. We SO want to pull them out of it, to touch them, to hold them, to talk with them. But we can't. A few years ago, I was in a store that had 3-D pictures in a plastic cube. Just bring in your photograph and they could etch it inside the cube. I'm still tempted to do that with a picture of Phil, so I can really "see" him again. But as yet, I haven't done it. Mostly, I talk to Phil's picture, and tell him that I love him. The feeling of wanting to pull him out of the picture seems to have subsided, but I believe we will always look long and hard at our loved one's pictures from time to time. Their pictures are also a good way of "introducing" them to the family that never

Left: My Aunt Charmaine in 1941
Above: Phil and
his dog Dackel in 2001

had the privilege of walking on this earth with them. I "met" my aunt that way. My dad's sister went Home at the age of 14, when my dad was seven. I only knew my Aunt Charmaine by the picture my grandma always had displayed of her. Charmaine stood there with her 1940's hairdo, her ice skating outfit, and her skates perfectly laced up. I listened to stories of her life, and her death from my grandma, and I cherished getting to know an aunt that I will meet one day in Heaven. I do the same for our grandchildren, introducing them to Uncle Phil through his photographs and stories.

I imagine all people grieve differently. I tend to feel the tears more at night, as I grow tired and my defenses are depleted. That's when my "nourishment" for the day is running low.

Rest is SO VERY IMPORTANT! Even now, 12 years later, I am still a mom who misses her son. Because of that, even though a great healing has taken place, my eyes can start to "water" when I get overly tired. Recently, a friend had major surgery. She is also a mom with a child in Heaven. She was concerned because of the emotions she was feeling, and the tears that would seem to come out of nowhere. I talked with her about it, and reminded her that surgery makes us very tired, and with a child in Heaven, the missing can cause us to get teary. It will feel like grief, probably because it is. It's not that we aren't living fully again, and at peace with what God has brought us through. It's because we will always miss our children. I don't have the stamina emotionally and physically that I once had before Phil went Home. I didn't know if my stamina would return eventually. It doesn't seem to have. I am more sensitive now. I have more limits on my time and my energy now. I can't/don't push myself like I once did. And, it's really okay. Quiet and rest with God is a good thing in this busy world. To refocus is not harmful; it is filled with growth and a new strength in Christ alone.

I'm sleeping okay. But when I wake up, no matter what time it is, I'm usually done sleeping. My mind starts to "think," and the reality comes back.

Sleep, in the beginning, seemed to be the only way to really escape the harsh reality of what had happened in saying good-bye to Phil. It got to the point where I didn't even want my husband to wake me up with a kiss good-bye in the morning if I was still sleeping. It would only make the pain return sooner. I asked him to please let me sleep as long as I was able. Then one night, many, many years later, I had a nightmare. In the nightmare, Phil was sick with Leukemia again. It was hard going, and a very pain-filled dream. When I woke the next morning, I was relieved that the nightmare was over. It was then that I realized my day-time nightmare was no longer what it once was. I realized a great healing had taken place. I could now wake up with a heart that didn't always hurt.

*The times when our hearts ache the most don't last too long. Just long enough to teach us that we need God, and He is our only source of peace. The minute I think my peace is found **anywhere** else, I quickly learn it is **not**.*

It's hard to believe, but there are moments, even early on when it seems all is still well with the world. Actually, early on it's easier. The reality hasn't fully set in yet. Our mind asks, "This couldn't really have happened, could it?" But those times don't last very long. Thinking "we" can really do this **without** supernatural, spiritual strength from above, or the power of the Holy Spirit within us, will quickly dissolve us into a puddle of tears. Our Father keeps calling us back into His loving arms to His comfort and Hope. If we are wise, we will go there often, and stay as long as we can.

We could bury them under busyness and a forced smile (as the "world" sometimes tell us to). But then I don't believe we would heal.

How many of us have heard, "Stay busy"? Probably all of us. It is not the way I found healing. Maybe it's because I am much more a Mary than a Martha. But I have to wonder if "busyness" really works for anyone on the path of healing? Having things to do is great. But if emotions are getting buried and not dealt with, they will only emerge later in other ways.

I don't want to get a few years down the road and find out that I've made little progress.

There are a lot of "dark rocks" to turn over and see what's underneath. We don't want to. We know that what we see there will hurt. For instance, driving down that road again will hurt. Going to that store again will hurt. Listening to that song again will hurt. Eating that food again will hurt. Watching that movie again will hurt. Let's face it, everything hurts the first time we attempt to do it without the one we love. But avoiding things doesn't cure what ails us. When the time is right, moving through all the things that hurt, one at a time, will cure our broken hearts. We will see that we can do it, we can watch it, we can listen to it, and we can eat it. I came home from work and my husband, Jim, had cooked up a box of dressing that Phil had chosen at the store. It had set in our cupboard for a few months. I wasn't about to cook it. I mentioned it to Jim when I saw it on the stove. He knew it. He had braved it. We ate it. It didn't kill us. What it does is break down the walls that Satan is trying to have us hide behind for the rest of our lives. It allows us to walk through "fire" without getting burned, and to help us not to fear that thing again in the future. One step, one experience, one *box of dressing* at a time. God will bring us through. Don't avoid. Instead, pray, and move forward in God's perfect timing.

I don't know how I'm supposed to grieve. I don't know what is correct, or what is even disrespectful. Will people think I didn't love my son if I smile?

Smiling is a very serious subject, for sure. When the smiles do come, go ahead and give it your all. You know how much you loved the person you are missing. The enemy lies to us and tells us it is wrong to smile again. What will people think? Well, people aren't thinking anything. We are! They are only hoping to see us smile again, one day. When that day comes, it will make everyone feel better. Don't worry. The tears will be right behind those first smiles, and many more to come. It has NOTHING to do with how much we love. It has everything to do with how much God loves us!

Phil didn't know of any of these plans, except that Dave would be doing his service.

Most times, we don't discuss what we will do when a person passes. Most times, we wait to make plans. We did the same. One day though, I talked with Phil about Pastor Dave doing his service. Phil agreed that would be fine. It's not losing hope for healing; it is respect for the person and what they want.

God's way is the healthy way. I have to believe that, because it is the only thing that brought Phil comfort in his final hours. And it is the only thing that brings me comfort now.

Ativan is given to those dying of cancer. It was given to Phil by his hospice nurse. The first time she came was the very day he went Home. She met him. She took his vitals. He was at peace knowing he didn't have to go into the hospital. With home care, he could stay in his own bed. It was what he wanted. But we never did use the Ativan he was given. We used God's Word. We sat by his bed and read to him. It calmed him. It calmed us. It was a good start to the grieving process. At one point, deep in my grief, I looked into the bathroom mirror. I said, "God, I can't stand this pain. If You want me to take something for this, I will. Maybe it will be so that I better understand others around me who need something. But I want You to get me through this." I never did take medication to relieve the pain of grief. I never did think about it much after that. But I know why some would need it. And I also know how being with God, in His Word, is very medicinal along the way.

It may take five years, or the rest of my life, but little by little I will grow stronger as He grows in me. When I empty my burdens on Him and allow Him to carry them, I breathe easier. That's all I need right now, to be able to breathe. The rest we will work on one day at a time.

Those who grieve know what I'm talking about. The very air we breathe is taken from us. I found myself taking in deep breaths, trying to get the air I needed. I didn't know how long that would last. I didn't know if I would ever breathe easy again. I didn't even know that I would grow stronger, but I surely hoped so. I **did** know that when I spent time with God, I could breathe easier for a time. I kept going back to Him for a new supply of "oxygen" in His Word and prayer. It worked! And today, 12 years later, my breathing is fine. I am stronger spiritually because my relationship with God is stronger. It is possible to make it through, and that's what's mostly on my heart in writing this book. I want to encourage **you** to hang in there with God. There's a good future that you have to look forward to in your own walk **through** grief and **beyond** with God's mighty healing power, and love!

Gift #6 – Rest is okay and even needed. Enjoy the quiet times.

What used to be easy, but now only seems possible with the power of God working in and through you?

Is it hard for you to have new limits on your stamina? Why or why not?

Record today's date and other notes you'd like to make:

The Great

<u>I AM</u>

Yes, my soul, find rest in God;
my hope comes from him.
Psalm 62:5 (NIV)

CHAPTER SEVEN

Why, my soul, are you downcast? Why so disturbed within me?
Put your hope in God, for I will yet praise him,
my Savior and my God.
Psalm 42:5 (NIV)

Me

Is it Finished?

Sunday, 02 Dec 2001

It is Sunday night, and my mind is a swirling mixture of emotions that won't die down. I'm exhausted beyond belief, yet unable to sleep. What am I to do with myself now? I really have no idea. I am almost afraid to let my mind go where it needs to. Will the pain at last be too much to bear? Will the reality of Phil being gone penetrate deeper than it has before, taking me to a level that I have not yet dealt with? And what will happen then? And who was that woman at his service? The one who was able to smile, and chat, and get through the entire proceedings in a way I never thought possible.

Pastor Dave talked about contradictions—a word I don't use often, and yet that was on my mind a lot throughout the evening. How different it all was from the graveside service; and yet how equally wonderful and God-filled! One was so quiet, so intimate, so perfect. The other, so quiet, so intimate, so perfect in my heart. Though there were so many of you there to share in this celebration of Phil's life, it did not distract from the intimacy I felt in my heart. How could it, with the love that was present?

There are no words to express what I feel and I'm sure what Jim feels in his heart, about Phil's service and all the loving hands that came together to give God the glory as we celebrated Phil's life. I only desired two things on Saturday evening: that God would get the glory, and that those there would come to know Phil, maybe for the first time, maybe a little bit better, or maybe in a way they never knew him. Did this happen? I feel that it did. But I'm still not thinking entirely clear like I would like to. God's protective fog encircles me with gentleness, I think, so that a mother's heart will not break into a thousand pieces.

I just cannot absorb the total reality that he is gone. And I'm still not able to absorb the massive amount of love that helped to "finish" the last details of Phil's life. But is it the finish, or merely the beginning of the impact he will have on me, on our family, and on everyone who reads the words I will write about this experience?

I never know when I'm going to write, what I'm going to write, or if I will ever write again. Sometimes I feel as if there is nothing left to say, and then my heart fills up and it needs to vent. This is one of those times. But how ironic, when there really are no words, and yet words are the only "tool" I have to express what is inexpressible.

A young life is gone from this earth. A life I cherished so deeply that it is impossible for me to believe he is gone. A young life I now picture on the streets of Heaven, healthy, and happy. I try so hard to cling to that image, of how happy Phil is now. I want him back so badly. Phil's vacation is almost over, right? He'll be coming home soon? I think even his dog believes that as she wanders down the hall, turns into his room, looks around, and then turns to leave. He'll be coming home soon. He's been on many vacations before; we just need to wait until he returns. What does a dog do when the "vacation" is never over? What does a mother do? Maybe a dog will switch its loyalties. She certainly is loved enough by Phil's brothers to do that. Time will tell...

But what does a mother do? I don't know yet. I know that God is all mighty, and all powerful. I know that when I got ready on Saturday afternoon to go to the service, I didn't think I could handle it. But just retreating to my room, and reading the Psalms, praying for help and strength, God picked this woman up and carried me from that point on. He gave me an excited peace for what the evening held.

As we were driving to the service, I was looking forward to it but said I wish it were for someone else. Then it dawned on me what I had just said, and that's not what I meant at all. I don't wish this on anyone.

Upon arriving at our church, the preparations were well under way—almost completely done. Many family members had already arrived, and many of our extended family (church members) were tending to all that needed to be done. It all looked beautiful. It was a well orchestrated movement of everyone using their gifts to bring this evening together.

All I could do was hug, hug, hug, and thank, thank, thank. Where were the tears? I think they were so covered with joy and love that they were invisible. I was so grateful for what was being done, and for all who would come to something that most envision as "not fun," but a "duty," yet come anyway. Friends and family come because that's what we do. We laugh together, and we mourn together. That's how life is.

For those that were there, you saw and experienced this celebration. For those that were not able to be there, I wish you could have shared this evening with us. I think it was unusual, but I'm not even totally clear on that yet. In fact, on Sunday morning I woke up thinking and saying, "I don't know...I don't know..." My best friend, Deb, asked me, "What don't you know?" I said, "I don't know..."

Later in the morning, I glimpsed the end of the service on video. Pastor Dave was talking, and it was like, "Oh, okay. I think it's okay." Thank you, Dave, for hurting with us; for being with us through our most difficult days, and for being a friend as well as a pastor. Thank you for caring so, so much. You have blessed us!

Maybe if this had been a normal funeral, I wouldn't have been saying "I don't know." But it wasn't a "normal" funeral. This was a celebration of Phil's life—everywhere. There were table center pieces with his hats and toys. There was a memory table that represented all his "loves." Coffee was brewing, food was arriving, there were flowers, and candles lit. There was music playing, programs being distributed. The entire church had been transformed from a women's tea in the afternoon, to Phil's service within a short period of time. Stories were told, communion was celebrated, songs were sung, and pictures of his life were enjoyed. We sat there, in the front row, partaking of this celebration. We as his parents, his brothers, his family and friends; watching his life flash before our eyes. And we turned our mourning, into dancing, literally.

I've never done that at a service before. Is this what God wanted? I have to believe He did, because it came together with great ease. We wanted to share our Hope in Jesus. We wanted everyone to know that God is good; that He takes good care of us, and that He took good care of Phil. We wanted everyone to know that Phil was loved; that we took good care of him, and that we would do anything for him, whatever it took. And we wanted everyone to know that there is still joy in our hearts, and that our mourning will eventually turn into dancing. And even now, we get glimpses of that.

We wanted to celebrate communion. Because without that, we might as well all go home and cry. If Christ did not die for us, and there was no resurrection, then there would be no seeing Phil again, and there would be no reason to celebrate ANYTHING! But Phil believed in Christ. He hung onto that Hope with his dying breath, and so will we. Yes, we believe in things we have not seen. We hope for things we cannot grasp yet, and we will continue to do so.

After seeing all that God has done for us through this long ordeal, and after watching Phil take this journey with a peace that does transcend understanding, how can we not believe in God's great love? God carried our boy Home in His loving arms, and God will carry us as we slowly absorb this reality.

The stories in the Bible tell of all the great things God has done for His people. The stories in our lives tell us of all the great things God has done for us. We cling to those stories, and work hard to remember them when we start to wonder, "Where is God?" He is right here. We just need to open our hearts to what He is doing, and then we will see Him clearly; more clearly than I see the reality of this situation right now.

I see God answering every prayer, every need that we, as a hurting family, might have. We ask God for His help, and depend on it. Our Father won't force His way into this if we try to do it on our own. We know that. But after what we have witnessed, why would we even want to try?

I know, I, for one, cannot do this without God. You saw me there. You visited with me. Who was that woman? That was a mother whose heart is broken, but who felt no pain, because I prayed to God to help me in my distress; to let His light shine on my face and sustain me. And He did. I don't really understand that kind of power, but I trust it, because I've seen it work. I rely on it, and will continue to do so, so that when the reality of Phil not being on "vacation" sinks into the core of my being, I will be able to stand tall and say, "God is good, all the time." He will turn our mourning into dancing, if we will just let Him. One day at a time. One hour at a time. One prayer at a time. I choose that!

There are times when I just say, "I can't stand this. I don't want to do this anymore!" But there is no choice. This is it! This is what we must do. And I can only pray that God will give me a willing spirit to sustain me. He is faithful.

Finished? I think it's only just begun. Saturday night might have been the closing of a chapter in the life of Philip Andrew Shore, but there is much more to come. As we heal, we will learn. As we learn, we will grow. Someday, we will look back and see how far we've come. Right now I look forward, and see how far we have to go. God help us!

Cast all your anxiety on him because he cares for you.
1 Peter 5:7 (NIV)

Good night,
Diane

==

Hello All,

God does not give me the gift of writing, as he does with Diane. He gives other gifts to me. As always, though, Diane's words express what I am feeling also. This is why I forward this to you, with love.

I cannot thank all of you enough! I know you are out there thinking of us, praying for us. And even if you couldn't physically be with us, you were still with us. Remember: "For to me, to live is Christ, to die is gain" Philippians 1:21 (NIV)
In His grip, Jim

Myself

What am I to do with myself now? I really have no idea. I am almost afraid to let my mind go where it needs to. Will the pain at last be too much to bear? Will the reality of Phil being gone penetrate deeper than it has before, taking me to a level that I have not yet dealt with? And what will happen then? And who was that woman at his service?

There certainly were a lot of unanswered questions on that day. What would it have looked like if I could have pulled up a chair, and shared a cup of coffee with "Me" then? What would I have said? Now, I know, I would mostly listen. That's what's most important; to *listen* to a broken heart full of questions, to pray, and hug, then really **listen** again, and pray, and hug again. But since these writings are to speak to **Me** from where **Myself** is now, I will. I want to reassure **Me** that God is with us. He will show us what to do *each* step of the way. Trying to figure it all out, and plan it all out now, is just not possible. There are too many moments, in too many days, to even try to know what it is going to look like. Eventually, our mind *will* go where it needs to, and it *will* be too much to bear without God in the midst of the pain. I disagree that God doesn't give us more than we can handle. This was more than I could handle alone without God's strength. The reality of our loved one being gone *will* penetrate much deeper through the months and years. I don't say that in a discouraging way, but in a real way. How can it not penetrate deeper as we begin to walk out the steps of living a life that doesn't include their physical being? And what happens then? We either learn how to avoid the reality of it by not talking about it, by not grieving deeply for them, by stuffing it deep down inside and trying to live with the intense pain; or we talk about what has happened with those we trust, and with God. And we grieve deeply, freely, and for quite a long time. We bring all the pain we are feeling to the surface, we hand it over to God, and we ask Him to help us deal with it, to live with it, and to live through it. *And what will happen then?* We *will* live through it! And we will begin to understand the power God

66

has to heal us. We will begin to rely on our Lord every single day of our life and know the blessing of mourning. At first, mourning will feel like a curse. But much, much later on, we can begin to understand that God's Grace is truly sufficient for the "thorn" we must forever live with. And 12 years later, **Me**, you will become that woman at the service, who could smile, and hug, and find the strength to do and be what God calls you to. And you WILL BE AMAZED at how awesome and mighty God's healing power really is. But in the beginning **Me,** you must grieve. And that is okay. It will get better. God promises us that when we give our whole heart to Jesus.

Though there were so many of you there to share in this celebration of Phil's life, it did not distract from the intimacy I felt in my heart. How could it, with the love that was present?

God's love is penetrating. He pours His love into our lives in so many ways. I truly appreciated all those who were there in our time of need. But mostly, I truly appreciate how God has it planned to use each and every one in such an amazing way. So many gifted people came together to make Phil's celebration service just what it needed to be. Paula was receiving food, Emily was taking pictures, Annet was setting up Phil's memory table, Vera was organizing things, Kim and Karen were handing out programs, Ron was making sure the church was just as it should be. The list is many as friends sang, played instruments, served, designed center pieces, cooked, loved on us, prayed for us, and took care of every bit of what was needed. God worked it all out. We could not have. We weren't thinking clearly. We were only moving forward because God's strength made it possible. When Phil was on his last day, and his Hospice nurse walked into his bedroom, she exclaimed, "There is so much love in this room!" It took me by surprise. We had been in his room; we must have been used to the enormous amount of God's love that filled that small space. But she felt it. I remember thinking, "We are only caring for our child as any parent would in this circumstance." But she wasn't talking about our love; she was talking about the Love that surrounds us and is poured through us by the Holy Spirit. She experienced it on that day, and we experienced it on the day of Phil's celebration service.

I only desired two things on Saturday evening; that God would get the glory, and that those there would come to know Phil, maybe for the first time, maybe a little bit better, or maybe in a way they never knew him. Did this happen?

When someone has been sick a long time, they begin to not really look or act like themselves. There were times during Phil's illness when his meds would start to wear off, and his sense of humor would return. I would catch glimpses of the son I knew him to be. So many didn't get to know him like that, and that's what we wanted to share with people. We wanted everyone to know that there was more there than just a person who has gone Home. Phil is a person we would have liked you to know. And through knowing Phil, we would also like you to know how great is our God! If a celebration of life can fulfill those two things, I believe it is a very good thing. And I believe many remember Phil's service in just that way. How thankful we are.

But is it the finish, or merely the beginning of the impact he will have on me, on our family, and on everyone who reads the words I will write about this experience?

This seems like a strange question now. But at the time, it seemed like we were finishing up so much. Five and a half years of our life had totally changed after Phil's initial diagnosis. I have been asked more than once through the years, which might be preferred; to have a child die suddenly, or to have years to start saying our good-byes? The answer to that question is not really in the "way" a child, or any loved one leaves us, as much as it is in the aftermath of their departure. It doesn't matter if we have an idea ahead of time of what is to come, or if we are taken totally off guard. It is the same hole once they are gone. It is the same grief. It is the same learning to live again without them. It WILL have an impact forever, personally, and on our families. The real question is, "What kind of impact will it have?" That is to be determined by how much we are willing to trust God, and let go in the process. Those are personal choices we will make every day for the rest of our lives.

I never know when I'm going to write, or what I'm going to write, or if I will ever write again? Sometimes I feel as if there is nothing left to say.

I feel that very same way just writing this book. I wonder, how can I possibly write an entire book answering **Me** with **Myself** now? We shall see. If you're holding a finished book in your hand, that answers that question. But that question is yet to be answered by **Myself** on this day.

I want him back so badly. Phil's vacation is almost over right? He'll be coming home soon? I think even his dog believes that as she wanders down the hall, turns into his room, looks around, and then turns to leave. He'll be coming home soon. He's been on many vacations before; we just need to wait until he returns. What does a dog do when the "vacation" is never over? What does a mother do?

It does seem impossible, unbelievable, and reversible somehow. But it isn't. As I was talking with a friend this morning about death and divorce, I almost think divorce is harder in some ways. Death is final on this earth. We HAVE to adjust to not seeing that person again. Divorce leaves that person out there to be seen, and that can be more torturous. But eventually, we do learn to adjust, and go on with life. Even Phil's dog, Dackel, did. The first year she was depressed. Seriously, she was. A lot of her hair fell out, and she lost weight. This was not because the rest of the family did not love her. But somehow she knew Phil was gone from her, and she missed him. Just moments after Phil went Home, Dackel jumped on his bed, walked over to his still body to lick him, and then turned and left before doing so. Normally, she would have been all over him. But she could tell he was no longer there. After about a year, Phil's Dachshund started to come back to us. Dackel was later lovingly adopted by Phil's cousins, and lived a long healthy life as a country dog. But every time we would visit her, she knew deep inside we were "home." My sister-in-law, Sandra, said that when we would leave, she would whine by the door like with no other company who had been there. Dackel was very happy and very well taken care of, but I think she always thought we'd be taking her back to Phil. I know there are animals in Heaven. So I have to believe that they are together once again.

My best friend, Deb, asked me, "What don't you know?" I said, "I don't know..."

I didn't know, what I didn't know. I think now I just wanted everything to have been what it should have been. I think watching the video of the service helped a lot. God's protective comforting fog so covered me on Saturday, that when I woke up on Sunday, I wasn't sure of all that had transpired. It left me confused. It is good to have recordings to go back and see/listen to later on.

I've never done that at a service before. Is this what God wanted? I have to believe He did, because it came together with great ease.

Putting Phil's service together, looking back now, is amazing to me. Jim and I sat and listened to music, and we picked out the songs we thought would be good. We gave that list of songs to the worship team at church in the order we wanted them played. It started out very somber with, "As the Deer (Pants for Water)" and finished with an upbeat song about God turning our mourning into dancing. Jim had played percussion with the worship team at church, and when that last song began, he couldn't help but walk up onto the stage and join in with them. Everyone there was on their feet, clapping and singing! We have been told since, by some on the worship team, that it was the most fun "funeral" service they had ever done. When we first gave the leader the music, he didn't know quite what to think. Well, neither did we. But God did. God put that service together to show exactly what I am writing about here today; the progression of grief, from mourning to dancing!

We wanted to celebrate communion. Because without that, we might as well all go home and cry.

This is our HOPE. Our only HOPE! If you don't know Jesus, you can invite Him into your life today. (See page 250.)

There are times when I just say, "I can't stand this. I don't want to do this anymore!" But there is no choice.

I repeated that many times through the years. I couldn't stand it. It **was** too much! I wanted out, somehow. I wanted to bang my head against the big brick wall of grief, have it come tumbling down, and have Phil standing there behind it. But that doesn't work. There was no choice about what had happened. But there was a choice about what would happen next. I realize that more than ever on this day, 12 years later. Stephen Arterburn has written that *healing is a choice*. It is. And we had to choose it over, and over, and over again through the years, with every obstacle we faced. If we do choose healing, we will come through the darkness, and God will get the glory He is so deserving of. Jesus asked the man by the pool if he wanted to get well? Jesus knew it was a choice the man had to make.

Someday, we will look back and see how far we've come. Right now I look forward, and see how far we have to go. God help us!

And God did! Our Lord helped us get 12 years down the road. In no way shape or form do I want to be where I was when I wrote that line 12 years ago. And I'm so sorry if that is where you are on this day. That is my biggest sorrow. When I hear of someone who has just entered into the grief walk, it hurts my heart. I know that good things will come, but I also know the way is long, and it is hard. It just is. That's why I MUST tell you, it WILL get better! It WILL, with God's help. Years ago I met with a father whose son had been shot to death the night before. We listened to his story, and we prayed with him. When we were done, he said, "I guess it's just one day at a time now." I said, "No, it's one moment at a time." It is, especially early on. We have to open up our hemorrhaging heart to God's healing touch, one moment at a time. One day, you can laugh again. You can live again. You can even thrive!

Gift #7 – Discovering the moment-by-moment healing power of our Mighty God!

What seems most impossible about God bringing you through this time?

Have you ever experienced a healing of any type from our Lord?

Record today's date and other notes you'd like to make:

The Great

<u>I AM</u>

Cast all your anxiety on him
because he cares for you.
1 Peter 5:7 (NIV)

CHAPTER EIGHT

Let me hear joy and gladness;
let the bones you have crushed rejoice.
Psalm 51:8 (NIV)

<u>Me</u>

A Good Day

Friday, 07 Dec 2001

*I have such a thankful heart tonight for the good day that I have
had. It was a day that started out with a dream of Phil—a healthy
Phil, about ten years old. He and I were getting into an elevator
with his brothers, Jimm, and Chris. They were younger too. Phil
had an open Monopoly game in his hands, and as we walked into
the elevator I woke up. I woke up feeling good. I had seen Phil. It
had been over three weeks since I had spent time with him, and we
got to be together for a few brief moments. I felt sooo good!*

*I had asked God yesterday to help me remember Phil, before he
was sick. Help me to remember the boy who played, and was
healthy, and not just the boy who spent those 5½ years fighting the*

fight. And God gave me this dream. I will treasure it until the next one. I know there will be more.

*Then I had a good day at work. I still grew tired as the day wore on. But it was easier than yesterday. The tears were not so near the surface. And I came home to just relax, not to cry. After resting, we went out for pizza, husband Jim, Chris and I. It was nice and easier than it has been. I feel a bit of independence this evening that I have not felt lately. Jim seems a bit perplexed by it. I told him he should be happy. This is the old me, even if it's just a glimmer of the "me" I used to be. It feels good to come out from under my cozy "blanket" and spread my wings. To me, it means healing. I sat in the hot tub tonight and praised God. I thanked God for His goodness. And His joy filled me! I **can** feel good again. It's good to know that.*

I know also, that I will never be the same. I will be different. My friends and family may have to get acquainted with this new me. I don't think it will be bad, just different. I'll be a bit more reserved maybe, more reflective, more willing to take in the surroundings and quietly absorb them, rather than bulldoze through things I might have before.

*When I find myself leaning forward, and trying to make headway on my own, I find God asking me to lean back. He wants me to lean back into His arms and relax. He wants me to let **Him** do the work. When I do, I feel better. I want to take things slowly, but I want to heal as quickly as possible, too. I'm finding that means I must move as God directs. I have to take time to relax, to sleep, to eat, to pray, to read God's word, to listen to good music, and enjoy the good moments. If I move too fast, I get too tired, and then I hurt too badly. The ache becomes too much then, and I'm drawn to Phil's picture, wanting to grab his face out of it and hold him. That becomes **unbearable**. I don't want to feel that way. I want to be quiet, and remember Phil. I want to heal from the pain of missing him, so that one day I can remember his whole life—all the good days, as well as the hard ones. He deserves that. He lived a full* *life, not just a sick one. I don't want my memory to be clouded with just the sick days and heartache.*

We watched the video of Phil's Celebration Service again. Of course I saw things I had not seen before, and I enjoyed it. It was meaningful, and touching, and joyful. Phil would have liked the Weird Al songs during the video of his life. I know he would have laughed. He loved Weird Al's music. He even got to meet him backstage after one of his concerts. I'm glad his service is over, but I'm glad for what it was. It will always be a good memory for me, in so many ways.

Good memories. Life is full of them. I remember my grandma talking about her memories. She lived through so much, and yet she was so joyful. I'm understanding her better now, and why her relationship with God was what sustained her. It's good to know she is in Heaven with Phil. They will get along great!

*Our son...what an impact he has had on my life, and continues to have. Pastor Dave said he was a sprinter, while we're running a marathon. It seems like he was here and gone so quickly. So I guess he was a sprinter. Where did his sixteen years go? The years went by so fast. I hope I, too, will be saying, "Where did the years go?" in years down the road when the smiles come more easily than the tears. I'm sure I will. But today, it has been three weeks and two days, and I feel joy and peace. I am **so** thankful.*

For those that don't hear from me—for those e-mails that I haven't responded to, or those phone calls that I haven't returned—it's not because I don't care, or I'm not interested. Right now, I'm just moving at a snail's pace. And even when my mind says I need to do something, my body says rest. So I do. I hope you understand. There will be time in the future, God willing. But for now, I must rest, and heal, so I can be and do whatever God calls me to do with the rest of my life. It's exciting to think about what that may be. But it must be in God's timing. I'll leave you with a poem:

Both Our Sons

Oh Lord I have the time now, there's so much I could do
But I move just like a snail, leaning back on You
I want to move too quickly, sometimes I think I should
But You gently remind me, it's time to heal, for if I would
Run ahead too quickly, plunge in where I see need
I might be greatly damaged, it might cause my heart to bleed
More than what's required, as I mourn for my dear son
It hurts enough right now, there's no reason to try and run
Faster than is necessary...
He says, *slow and easy child*
Your Father is in control, I'll lead you all the while
When these days are finished, and bones that have been crushed
Rejoice again, and praise Me, they'll be time then, please do trust
That future days are waiting, for all that you must do
For now relax and wait a bit, be still and be renewed
Let all the world around you, go on, it can't be stopped
But you can take your time, then in time you'll see you're not
Behind what I am asking, but right on track, you'll see
The more that you will trust Me, the more you'll be set free
To live the life you're called to, abiding in My love
Full of all the joy and peace, pouring down from up above
Hurting hearts can heal, that is a proven fact
But only in their own time, with My help and with My map

Ahh...You'll guide me to the finish, where the victory is won
Ending up in Heaven, yes there, with both our sons

<u>Myself</u>

*I had asked God yesterday to help me remember Phil, before he
was sick. And God gave me this dream. I will treasure it until the
next one. I know there will be more.*

And there have been many more dreams. And I still appreciate
each one. Not all of them make sense, but they are always a gift.

When we can't be with those we love, whether they are in Heaven or somewhere else on this earth, dreams can be nice.

Then I had a good day at work. I still grew tired as the day wore on, but it was easier than yesterday. The tears were not so near the surface.

To this day, I am surprised that I went back to work after only three weeks. It was probably because the type of job I had, allowed me to grieve. I worked at our church as the receptionist. Everyone was more than understanding. My manager, Kim, would allow me to leave whenever it got to be too much. I remember most days, I would cry all the way to work. Then I would be okay when I walked into work. But as the hours went by, I would start to gasp for air, literally. I started to need quiet. I started to need alone time with God. I would simply find Kim, and tell her I needed to go home. She would readily agree it was time. Then I would cry all the way home in my car. The days were difficult, to say the least. One day at work, I sat with about eight other people around a table in the break room. Everyone was talking about this or that. I could not join in. It was so draining. Eventually, I had to get up and go into the bathroom. I went into a stall, and stayed there until I could breathe again. It had nothing to do with anyone doing anything "wrong." It had everything to do with fresh grief. Those moments, I remember. But they are good to remember. They remind me that those days **don't** last forever. Now when I go to work at my new job, as a hair stylist, I not only have the strength to persevere through the day, but many times, I get to share all the good things that God has done, too. I am grateful for those opportunities. They are the highlight of my day!

This is the old me, even if it's just a glimmer of the "me" I used to be.

There were times, even early on, when there would be a spark of the healing that God was doing. Thinking about it now, these small glimmers seemed "huge" to me. But I'm sure to those around me, they could tell I had a very, very long way to go.

God's joy filled me! I can feel good again. It's good to know that.

Those moments of feeling good, even in the beginning, are okay to feel. They are surprising. And sometimes we feel guilty about them. But they are normal and needed. Sometimes, it seems we might never come up for air. It seems that we are held under a tidal wave so large we will surely drown. I believe God gives us just enough good moments as a reprieve, so we can know there can be better days ahead. There is a purpose in our suffering. It is written in James 1:1-4 (NIV), "Consider it pure joy, my brothers and sisters, whenever you face trials of many kinds, because you know that the testing of your faith produces perseverance. Let perseverance finish its work so that you may be mature and complete, not lacking anything." Grief definitely burns off certain parts of our character that aren't beneficial in serving in God's Kingdom work. We gain a greater Heavenly perspective in grief. Our focus shifts, and we learn to endure. In this world, endurance is a good quality to gain. There are many things we will go through before leaving here. God fills us with His strength, to make it through them all.

I know also, that I will never be the same.

We who grieve will **never** be the same. That is a given. But **how** we will be, is a choice. Some do, literally, drown in their sorrow—they are lost emotionally to those around them on this earth forever. That is very sad, but very true. It doesn't have to be that way though. God is bigger than death. God is bigger than grief. Jesus conquered the grave! As I once said in a talk I was giving, I have never read anywhere in the Bible where God says, "I have taken care of everything you need. I can handle it all. But the one thing I can't help you with is the death of your child." God promises that He is **for** us, and not against us. When we trust in His promises, they work. **God** works! We will never be the same, but we can be even better because we can know God better than ever before.

My friend, Barbara, of 40 years, waited for the "old" me to re-emerge. I never did. But I was also eventually able to be by her bedside when she went Home to Heaven. I was "not lacking anything" in that moment, because of the power of the Holy Spirit that lives inside of us as believers. I was able to encourage Barbara about what was ahead for her. I was not afraid of death. I was not afraid to talk with her about what Jesus had provided for all those who believe in His saving Grace. I was able to comfort her with the comfort I had been given. She and I were seeing God at work, **because** I was never the same again. I was grateful for all that God had brought me through. I believe in those moments, Barbara was grateful, too! The old me would have never had the strength to endure such a difficult moment with my friend. With Jesus living powerfully inside of us, all things are possible. The last thing Barbara said to me was, "I love you."

When I find myself leaning forward, and trying to make headway on my own, I find God asking me to lean back. He wants me to lean back into His arms and relax.

That is the best way I can describe the "position" needed to heal. Leaning forward was not where God wanted me. He wanted me in His arms of comfort. He knows how much our hearts are hurting. He is an understanding Father. He wants to console us. He's not saying, "It's no big thing." He grieves with us, just as Jesus wept for His friend, Lazarus. Not because there is no Hope, but because there **is**—God wants us to reach for Him in our pain and find **His** Hope and live again.

I want to be quiet, and remember Phil. I want to heal from the pain of missing him, so that one day I can remember his whole life.

I had a long way to go, and a long time to get there, as all do who grieve. But way down the road, the harsh bumps start to smooth over. The pot holes are filled in. The scary curves straighten out. And the road became easier to navigate. I started to see there was only one direction to go, and that was and is straight toward our

God. Detours away from that straight road need to eventually be avoided. They only cause us more misery. They delay our journey.

One of Phil's best friends, Kendra, gave me a gift that said, "The memories we drag, become the treasures we carry." The memories aren't heavy 12 years later, they are precious. They can still bring an unexpected tear sometimes, as they did in church this very morning during one of our worship songs. But not to worry, they are sweet tears that God is collecting. Nothing is lost on our Savior.

He deserves that. He lived a full life, not just a sick one.

In going through picture albums just the other day, I was amazed at how many there were! I was also a bit sad for a few moments. The missing started to get a strong hold of me again. And then I stopped. Or perhaps, God stopped me. And I thought, "Wait a minute! I am THANKFUL for all the pictures, and all the things we did together!" Phil lived a very full life. He lived a very fun life, in the midst of all the suffering. It wasn't perfect, and it was a struggle, but it was as good as it could have possibly been. I need to be thankful for all those pictures, and all those smiles, and all those experiences. Thank You, Jesus, for all You have done!

Where did his sixteen years go? The years went by so fast. I hope I will be saying that in years down the road too, when the smiles come more easily than the tears.

I wondered if I would make it a day, a week, a month, a year; and I'm **still** here. I have more wrinkles, more gray hair, more stories to tell, and six beautiful grandchildren to love! Jimm and Chris are grown men in their 30's, with beautiful wives, and great careers. Time has moved on, and so has the life we are living. Jim and I found out that marriages can survive. We have

been married 38 years now. Praise God! I have a new career after always being a stay-at-home mom—I went to Beauty School, and did more than drop out. I made it through, AND got a job! I even get to work in the business now with my friend, Rene', who helped me walk through many a dark day. We live in a new place now. We go to a new church. Life has changed. And the smiles are many. And the gratefulness in our hearts is immeasurable! I am astounded at what our loving God can do with a shattered heart. As they sang in church last Sunday, "You are all I need," I know those words to be true. I never would have known that without all that has happened. An easy life, unfortunately, doesn't teach us how much we need God and how He fulfills that need. Difficulties that help us to know our Savior up close and personal, come in very useful when the winds of life continue to beat against us in an untold number of ways—as they will until we, too, meet Jesus face to face.

For those that don't hear from me—for those e-mails that I haven't responded to, or those phone calls that I haven't returned—it's not because I don't care or I'm not interested.

I was very good at keeping up with correspondence, and sending out birthday cards, etc...before Phil went Home. That all fell to the wayside, for a long time, after Phil was gone. I can't say as I've even picked it all back up again. I know I haven't. Some things I am not as good at. Some things I am better at. I didn't clean house for 9 months. Jim's laundry, when done, sat in the garage on top of the machines. He never complained. He helped wherever he could. Some things that fell to the wayside in the beginning, haven't returned as before. It's not such a bad thing. Yes, I get laundry done now, and even put it away in the drawers. But I am much better at knowing when the work needs to be put aside, so time can be spent with those around me—like the day we were helping a man from our church move. I sorted and packed for a while, and then God stopped me, and asked me to talk with John for a while. We stood at the side of his house, and he shared his heart, and some tears with me. We prayed. I don't want to miss moments like that. I like that about grief. It brings to light what is most important, which is our relationship with God and others. We are

commanded to love the Lord our God, and others. Grief can help us learn to do that better.

Gift #8 – Our priorities can change, and for the better!

What have you been able to lay down for later, while you rest a bit?

What would you like to not pick up again, when your heart heals more?

Record today's date and other notes you'd like to make:

The Great

<u>I AM</u>

Jesus replied, "The most important commandment is this: 'Listen, O Israel! The LORD our God is the one and only LORD. And you must love the LORD your God with all your heart, all your soul, all your mind, and all your strength.' The second is equally important: 'Love your neighbor as yourself.' No other commandment is greater than these."
Mark 12:29-31(NLT)

CHAPTER NINE

Love must be sincere. Hate what is evil; cling to what is good.
Be devoted to one another in brotherly love. Honor one
another above yourselves. Never be lacking in zeal, but keep
your spiritual fervor, serving the Lord. Be joyful in hope,
patient in affliction, faithful in prayer. Share with
God's people who are in need. Practice hospitality.
Romans 12:9-13 (NIV)

Me

To Write or Not to Write...

Tuesday, 11 Dec 2001

To write or not to write...not me, you! I guess I'm surprised, in a
way, that some of you hesitate to write to me, or maybe even to
speak to me. It's another part of the puzzle that I'm trying to put
into place.

*Just as when Phil was sick, I still saw the boy **inside** the body that*
was bald and ill. To me he was just Phil, my son, who needed to be
loved and accepted. Maybe even some of the nurses entered Phil's

*room to care for his disease, not realizing who **he** was—just a child, needing to be cared for, not looked at or pitied, but just loved.*

Maybe that is me, now. I'm just a person who hurts, who longs for her son, who needs love and care and encouragement. Sometimes I feel "handicapped." Like some don't want to look at me. It's too uncomfortable for them. And yet, I'm just me, needing to be accepted and cared for; needing to not be different, but the same as you. We all hurt. We all have things we are dealing with—be it the loss of a loved one, financial difficulties, relationships that are estranged, health problems. We are a hurting world, needing our God and each other.

I truly believe God's love comes to us in many forms. It comes in the beauty of a sunset, the delicacy of a flower, the peace through trials, and the love of His people for one another. God's love flows through us to another and helps to heal what is hurting. It's like medicine on the wound, and my wound is deep right now. It needs lots of "medical" attention. It needs God's love poured through you into this wound, even when I am unable to respond.

*It's like Phil lying in his bed, needing our care, not able to help himself. He needed unconditional love poured upon him as he prepared to leave this world. He depended on us to help him while he waited for God to take him Home. He was totally relying on God and others—not that it would change anything. It was still his time to go Home. But with God and the love of those around him, he would be able to do it peacefully. We couldn't heal his "wound," just as you can't heal mine with words, or hugs, or cards, or anything. But we could help him along, just as you can help me along by all those acts of love. I don't just speak for myself. I speak for my family who are hurting, too. And I speak for all those you know who are hurting in whatever form. We **need** one another. And we need to be bolder in sharing with one another, instead of being so cautious because we're afraid to cause further harm. I have to believe that is rarely the case. There has not been one e-mail I have received, one card, one expression of* *sympathy that has caused me more pain. The pain is GREAT! It would take a major life earthquake for me to feel any further damage to my already damaged heart. Even if a wrong word was spoken, it would rate about 0.00000001 on the Richter scale. There is a 99.999999 percent chance of not offending me by talking with me. But by not saying anything, or not writing anything, or not acknowledging that tug on our hearts to help anyone in pain, there is a 99.999999 percent chance of not allowing God's love to flow through us to help another.*

I need to cling to God, right now as never before. There are times when I barely have the strength to ask God for help, but I can whisper a soft "help me." And He does. When you come to me, I am able to stay still and quiet and let God's love pour over me like a cool drink of water. It quenches my thirst. It refreshes my spirit, and helps me keep moving forward through the pain I feel. God uses his people to care for His people. Just as my writing, my pain, and my grieving being expressed through words may help you with something you might be dealing with, your acts of compassion help me.

When I write, I am simply allowing God to use me. When I share with you, what is very private to me, it is an act of obedience. There are times when I would rather not. What will you think? Will you think I'm a lunatic? A crazy woman? I share with you because I feel God calling me to do it. Perhaps He has given me the gift of writing to help others? I will not bury it under a rock. This is how I try to honor God, and worship Him, and allow Him to use me. Help me continue on by doing the same. I long to hear from you, especially if it helps me to know Phil's suffering is being used for God. I need to remember that EVERY DAY! It helps me get out of bed.

I know, now, why some people never recover from a loss like this. I'm a strong woman. I can bear pain. I can climb mountains, and ride my bike 100 miles in a day with barely a complaint. But I can't do this alone. I can't. I need you to be bold and help me! And I need God every second of every day as I pray to heal from this wound that bleeds so easily right now. So never think that you might say the wrong thing, and therefore remain silent. If you have the strength, right now, that I am needing, that others you know are needing, help them and help me. Be bold! Pray for what God would have you do. And then do it!

It's not like you will cause me to think of something that will be painful. I already think about it. I already think about Phil all day, every day. Mentioning his name will not bring him to mind and cause a tear. He is on my mind all the time, and I already shed those tears. I want to talk about him. I want to remember him and share all that he means to me. I want you to remember him and be glad that he lived, as I am.

*I write this, not just for me, but for everyone you know who's hurting. Help them through their trials by talking to them and praying for them, just as so many of you have already done for me and mine. And when the day comes when you need **our** help, maybe we will have learned how to do that by the example you have set.*

Thanks for "listening,"

Love, Diane

Myself

I'm just a person who hurts, who longs for her son, who needs love and care and encouragement.

This was a bold writing for me. Can you tell I was desperate? I was! I breathe in deep even now just thinking about this time. I needed everyone, and everything to make it through. This was not an angry message; this was a cry for help! No one knows what they are doing in times like these. I didn't. My friends and family didn't. I wanted to write about it so that we could get it out there on the table, and talk about it. So that there could be a comfort level, if that was at all possible. I know it's hard. I've been on the other side of grief, not knowing what to say. It's easier to avoid. But avoidance helps no one. If we know of nothing else to do, then simply give a hug, and say "I'm sorry." That's a start.

Sometimes I feel "handicapped."

It is a handicap. I realized that as the years went on. There is a part of us that has gone missing. It's like a soldier coming back from war with a missing leg or arm. It's a learning to live **without**, and it takes practice. A lot of practice!

God's love flows through us to another and helps to heal what is hurting. It's like medicine on the wound, and my wound is deep right now. It needs lots of "medical" attention. It needs God's love poured through you into this wound, even when I am unable to respond.

The truth is, we have no idea what someone needs, but God does. We have no idea what can change a moment in time, or change a day from sadness to joy, or even change a decision that can save a life. One of my friends was battling cancer. She was really struggling with the decision whether or not to take her own life. It *seemed* to her that no one really cared. That very day a meal arrived at her home, from someone at our church. It meant the world to her! It changed her perspective on her battle. It literally saved her life until God was ready, in His own timing, to take her Home. Her story has always reminded me just how important little acts of kindness are in our lives. No one has to save the world on their own, but we do have to save each other from feeling alone in this world.

—not that it would change anything. It was still his time to go Home.

Just as Phil went Home, so did my friend mentioned above. Life and death are just part of living in this fallen world. It isn't our responsibility to change those things, but we can do so much with our love in the process of living here. When others help us, we in turn learn to help others. Just like my granddaughter, Laila, who started kindergarten two days ago, we all have much to gain from being on the "playground" with each other. We can start to recognize others' needs, personalities, and gifts. God put this world together in such a way that it can still work while we wait eagerly for Jesus' return! But we have to show up in other people's lives and help out.

I can whisper a soft "help me." And He does. When you come to me, I am able to stay still and quiet and let God's love pour over me like a cool drink of water. It quenches my thirst. It refreshes my spirit, and helps me keep moving forward through the pain I feel.

In Phil's final hours, he was in his own bed. We wiped the sweat off his face, fed him ice chips, and read to him. He wasn't able to contribute anything to his care, and we didn't expect him to. It was his time to totally receive all that we could give to him. He was very sick, as was I when I wrote these words 12 years ago. I didn't even realize how sick/broken I was. When Phil made his last trip to the bathroom, just hours before he went Home to Heaven, he glanced into the mirror on his way out. I didn't want him to. He wasn't looking good, and I didn't want him to worry. Not worry? What a crazy thing to say even now. I guess what I am trying to say is, what was happening was out of his control, so fretting wasn't going to be of any help to him. With grief, it is out of our control in the beginning, also. The loss of life was in God's hands. The grief that comes to us after is equally in God's hands. But we have to be willing to leave it in His hands and let Him help us through. We can't exercise a leg that has a broken bone in the beginning. We have to cast it, rest it, and begin to walk on it again slowly, when the time is right. In the meantime, having others helping us is SO beneficial. In early grief, we need a lot of help. We have a severe "break." Later, we can start to walk more, using our own strength, with God as our support. Some say that Christianity is a crutch that weak people need to lean on. In the beginning, I didn't need just a crutch; I needed a **whole** hospital to get me through. Now, I continue to lean on God a great deal, because I know when I am weak, He is very, very, very strong!

What will you think? Will you think I'm a lunatic? A crazy woman?

I really didn't know what to think about the writing I did most of
the time. I didn't know how others would react. It was a scary
time, personally, and publicly with my writings. But I am here
today to say that honesty, while grieving, is essential; honesty with
God, and with others who are safe. Early on, there are lots of crazy
thoughts to work through. But God can handle them. I told God
how much I hated what had happened. I told Him that I couldn't
stand it! I told Him that I didn't want to do it! I complained, and
He listened. He understood, and He continued to love me through
it all. God never walked way from me. He never leaves us. But it is
very tempting to leave Him. It seems unfair! And it makes little
sense. We wonder if we have brought this upon ourselves
somehow? Honestly, we can't know the answers to all the
questions we have, but we can come to know God and trust Him
despite them.

Can I be really honest with you here? As the years have gone on,
something troubles me. I don't understand how we can live in
God's goodness and walk closely with Him during pleasurable
times, but then turn and totally abandon God when times get hard?
First of all, that's when we need our Father and Savior the most. It
doesn't make sense to turn away from our greatest Source of help.
But also, let's think about this for a moment... We are living our
lives, thinking God is all that is good, while someone across town
is sitting at the bedside of their dying loved one. Or we are
attending church and worshiping our God, giving Him all the
praise and glory, while someone in another country is living
through the horrendous aspects of war. And then, death comes to
our door, or tragedy strikes our family, and suddenly God is not
God anymore to us? Why, when it hits home, does it change who
God is? He hasn't changed one bit. He never changes like shifting
shadows. But we change our opinion of Him depending on our
circumstances. Does that make sense? I understand it, but it's not
right. I didn't give a lot of thought in my day to a clinic full of
precious children with balding heads, and nausea, and with blood
transfusions going on, until it became a part of our world. But

those children and their parents were always there fighting the good fight when our "good" life was going on, and we were loving God for His goodness. They are still there, EVERY DAY! It would be unfair of me to turn from God when chemotherapy became a part of our life. God was, and is, still the very same God.

I long to hear from you, especially if it helps me to know Phil's suffering is being used for God.

Nothing is more precious than hearing our loved-ones name on the lips of someone else. Even just yesterday I was out with my granddaughter having ice cream. We were talking about children in a family, and she said something about not having all boys or all girls. I told her that I had all boys. I had three of them. I asked her if she knew their names. She said, "Yes. Uncle Phil. Uncle Jimm. And my Daddy." I smiled. It was good to hear all three sons mentioned.

My Grandma taught me so much about how to go on living after a child has left us. She had two daughters die in childbirth, and one daughter die at the age of 14. My dad was her only remaining child. She may have wondered, "Why God?" And I can't say as she ever got the answer to that question, but I do know I have one of the answers. She paved the way for me. She showed me how to go on living, with a strong faith in our Almighty Savior! Her suffering was used for good in my life. As her granddaughter, I hope and pray I can pass that same legacy on to my grandchildren. I want them to know that God has the strength to save our souls, both on this earth and forevermore. You may be walking out the grief you're feeling for someone that you love. You may be leaving a legacy that you will never know about until those grand reunions in Heaven. Just because we might not know the reasons why we are on this path, doesn't mean the reasons aren't there.

It's not like you will cause me to think of something that will be painful. I already think about it.

I thought about Phil night and day, for a long, long, very long time. Everywhere we go, we will see reminders, and most people won't even be aware of it. Mentioning their name will not bring them to mind, they are already on our minds. But it can be a blessing to open up a conversation that might include them. One night, having dinner at a friend's house, the conversation flowed. Her grown daughters were there, her new husband was there, but her son was not. He was in Heaven. No one spoke of Jacob at the table—not even me. But later that night, I sent her a message. I told her that I was thinking of Jacob at the table, too, because I knew that she was. I wanted her to know that she was not alone in her thoughts. I don't know what that meant to her. But I do know what it would have meant to me. It's important!

I write this, not just for me, but for everyone you know who's hurting. Help them through their trials by talking to them and praying for them, just as so many of you have already done for me and mine.

I don't write what I write just for me. Granted, it has helped me tremendously along the way, to write it out. But I would like to think that others can benefit from all these words. I would like to think that some life, somewhere, will be touched because grief is understood just a little bit more through these stories. If we stop and talk to anyone, anywhere, they have a story to share and a hurt buried somewhere in their life. We are not alone on our painful journeys, although our enemy, the Devil, would like us to think so. Our enemy knows that when we gather together as believers in Christ, sharing our hearts, we are a strong fortress that he cannot easily penetrate!

Gift #9 – Understanding that Jesus came to rescue us, and we can help each other, too!

Have you experienced the help of friends and family in your deepest need? How? How have you not?

Have you, or are you beginning to, walk with others through their most trying times?

Record today's date and other notes you'd like to make:

The Great

I AM

May the God who gives endurance and encouragement give you the same attitude of mind toward each other that Christ Jesus had...
Romans 15:5 (NIV)

CHAPTER TEN

In her deep anguish Hannah prayed to the Lord, weeping bitterly.
1 Samuel 1:10 (NIV)

<u>Me</u>

Sadness
The 14th to the 14th

Saturday, 15 Dec 2001

I can still go into Phil's room and smell him. I can bury my face in his bedspread and drink in my son. He's almost here. He could be in the other room, watching Saturday cartoons like he used to do. But he's not. It's been a month...a full month. The e-mails with the Scriptures you sent are still there on his bed. A card from his friend that arrived after he went Home, is still there, unopened. His glasses are still on his dresser, along with his watch, and his wallet. Everything from his memory table has been put back into place and pictures hung back on his walls. It's all very neat, just sitting there, waiting to be visited by whoever might walk by and glance in. It's a good place to go from time to time, to be "with" Phil and remember him. I will keep it that way for now. There's no need to hurry and change anything. I might regret it if I move too quickly. I think I will know when it is time to change things. God will let me know; and He lets me know that now is too soon.

Last night I was so sad, just so sad. Was it because it had been one month? I don't think so, but maybe. Maybe I was just over-tired, or maybe it was just time to wash the wound clean with a flowing of tears—wash out anything that might build up and cause unneeded scarring. I found in the middle of my crying, and my anguish, that I would not die. This would not kill me. I've heard the only way out is to go through. I believe that's true. I think I was a bit disappointed to learn that it would not kill me. Maybe if I cry enough God will take me Home too? But no. I know that's not right. It's not my time. I think maybe I'm running a marathon, and I'm carrying a baton that needs to be passed on. Lessons learned, and faith shared. I can do that. I can do what God is calling me to do, with His strength. People say I'm strong. But I'm not. I'm weaker than I've ever been, and happy to be so. I'm happy to let God carry me, and He is amazing me. I pray, and I pray, and He answers my call. God carries me in public, He helps me to share about Phil, and He lets me grieve mostly in private. God knows me. He knows what I need, and when I need it, and He allows for that. Everyone's grief must be so different—as different as all our personalities. Even death must be so different. I hope that each death can be seen as clearly as we seem to see Phil's now. His life was such a perfect package of God working. His sixteen years were here and gone, it seems now, but so neatly tied up. We learned so much, and were able to finish the details our personalities needed to be satisfied. From afar, it may seem like a tragedy, but from within, it is seen as a gift, and our hearts are filled with gratitude. I heard about two men killed on a freeway in Florida, hit by an 18-wheeler. To me, it sounds so quick, so filled with unanswered questions as to why God would allow that? But to them, to their families, maybe they understand it? Maybe if they heard about Phil, they would think the same, and have unanswered questions? Maybe they would wonder why God would ever allow a 16 year old to die? We can't know all that God is doing. But I think those closest are given some light, if we open our eyes to it. I'm just wondering about these things. I hope you don't mind.

We have our Christmas tree up, and a few decorations around. It's going to be a simple Christmas, just quiet; probably just the four of us. We want it that way, or do I want it that way? Probably. I love people; I love to be around people. I love to visit, and laugh, and have fun. I've been doing a bit of that. But I love to be alone, also. That is how I re-energize. To be alone with God and my writing, feels good. I don't mean to be a recluse or rude, but I think this is what I'm supposed to be doing right now—capturing my thoughts and putting them down, so as not to miss each step along the way to healing. So maybe I can help someone else along this path. Maybe they will read my thoughts and not feel so alone. Maybe they will know then that the anguish won't kill them, and that being alone is okay if that's what they choose. Maybe as I find the way out by going through it, I'll take them along with me, and they'll find the way out also—especially if someone has gotten stuck in the darkness.

I don't plan on getting stuck in the darkness. I want to heal, and I know it will take time. But I will heal. Yes, I'm stubborn and hard-headed, and God knows that about me. Maybe that's why He chose me to write about this? Maybe God knew I would not give up, no matter how much it hurt? I have a magnet on my refrigerator from my friend Cheryl that says, "I would give up chocolate, but I'm not a quitter." That's me! There's a job to do, and it will get done, no matter how long it takes. There is a light at the end of the tunnel, even here on earth. Phil saw that light, and he was angry when it didn't take him Home for good. He was angry that he ended up back in his own bed, having thought he'd arrived in Heaven. I see that light here on earth too. I see a finish line down the road that's lit and calling to me. Walk this way, or run this way, but keep going in that direction, following after the One who knows the way. The less I stumble, and the less I detour, the more satisfying this race will be–filled with all the good things that God has planned along the way. Bring it on God! I'm looking forward to

the rest of the life You have planned for me. I'm looking to You,
and hanging on with all the strength You give me!

Face to face

This life can be so bumpy, so filled with fear and dread
The tears can fall so quickly, the darkness can easily spread
But I don't want that darkness, I want the gift of joy
I want to see God working, and I want to truly enjoy
All that God is doing, all that He has planned
For the life I'm living, I want to let Him expand
Upon the life I'm living, so when my race is run
He will welcome me Home, being greeted by His Son
I want to also hear the words, well done my chosen child
You had your share of heartaches, but you trusted all the while
And you kept your focus on Me, where it should be
You didn't let the evil one, lie to you foolishly
I want to know the life I live, is going where it should
I want to follow the right path, not wander through the woods
I want to cross the finish line, arms raised and banners flying
Glad for what's behind me, to arrive where there's no crying
I want to be an athlete, that draws upon God's strength
Not just one who works at it, but one who works by faith
I know that it is possible, because I'm not the first
And I won't be the last, to feel all this hurt
But maybe by my hurting, and running out this race
Others will want to follow Jesus, and meet Him face to face
That alone is my prayer, for He is our only Hope
I cling to all His promises, each day He helps me cope

Thank you for continuing to pray for us. We need all your prayers.
Prayer is so powerful! When Phil had had enough, when he finally
looked at me and said, "Mom, I don't want to do this anymore. Is it
okay to ask God?" I said it was, and we prayed for God to take
him Home. He went Home to Heaven within a few hours, after 5½
years of fighting this fight. Was God listening to this young boy,
and to his mother? You bet He was! And He heard our prayer and
He answered it. He hears all our prayers, even when it seems we

don't get answers right away. God's timing is perfect.
Thanks so much,
Diane

__Myself__

I can still go into Phil's room and smell him. I can bury my face in his bedspread and drink in my son.

Phil's room is long gone. It's all been dismantled, put away, given away, some of his things even sold in yard sales. It seems disrespectful to even write that, but it's true. If I had it to do over, I wouldn't recommend the yard sale part. It was just **so** painful—to see his toys being bought for a quarter, to watch someone walk away with his roller blades. But what are we to do with so many belongings that belong to no one anymore? It's a tough call, but one that must be dealt with at some point in some way. It's a personal decision. One sweet thing is to give a little something to friends and relatives—we did that too. They appreciate it so much!

I think I will know when it is time to change things. God will let me know; and He lets me know that now is too soon.

God did let me know when that "some point" had come. Did that make it any less painful? I don't really think so, but God did give me the strength to go through Phil's room when it needed to be done. It was good to keep it for a time though. It was a good place to go and grieve, and to draw close to Phil for a bit. A person's smell does linger on, and smells can be powerful, just as an old song can take us to a certain place in time. God allows for us to grieve, to smell, and to draw close. God allows our hearts to heal slowly. There is no rush when we are on His time table, and not our own. We have to constantly be seeking God on our journey, and listening for the Holy Spirit's instructions. It is the ONLY way to make it through.

I found in the middle of my crying, and my anguish, that I would not die. This would not kill me.

Boy, it seemed that it would. When a heart is literally breaking, it hurts, physically. It aches all day long, for a long time. I never knew that. But I found it to be true. My friend, Ann, asked me the other day if it is painful to go back through all these emotions again in writing this book. She wondered if it still hurts? I thought about it, and it's more like with childbirth. We can tell our stories with each child we have had. That's what young mothers do a lot. And even many years later when our children are grown, we remember the pain, we know it hurt a lot (especially without medication), and we can explain it, but we no longer actually feel the physical pain. When someone else is birthing a child, we know what they are going through, because we have been there, and we feel for them. That is how I feel when I hear of another child who has gone Home to Heaven. I feel for the parents in such pain, but I don't actually feel the physical pain anymore. I am grateful that God takes the pain away, but leaves the *knowing* so we can have compassion for another in that position.

I think maybe I'm running a marathon, and I'm carrying a baton that needs to be passed on. Lessons learned, and faith shared. I can do that. I can do what God is calling me to do, with His strength.

Phil was a sprinter. Pastor Dave said that at his service. Sixteen years, and whoosh, his race was run! I told Phil I'd probably be missing him for the next 40 years. It's been twelve, and I'm still running this race. I wrote that, "I can do what God is calling me to do." But how would I have known that at that time? It was probably written in ignorance. Ignorance is not a bad word; it simply means we don't know something. A lot of what I wrote was written because of Hope. Without Hope, I wouldn't have written anything at all, let alone the possibility of getting through such a horrific time. HOPE was the word I would cling to for most of the next 12 years. Now, I have moved on to the word LOVE. I believe eternal HOPE has been deeply embedded in my soul, and it now needs to be shared with tender LOVE.

Everyone's grief must be so different—as different as all our personalities.

Everything I write here is personal. You may relate to some of it, or none of it; but no one is going to relate to all of it. I hope that you can take what helps you, and discard the rest, or maybe use it for someone else you know. There are experts who have graduated with degrees in many of the things I am writing about. I don't have a degree, except from the *School of Hard Knocks* that some talk about. I only walked it all out as best I could, and I only write what I write now, as best I can.

We can't know all that God is doing. But I think those closest are given some light if we open our eyes to it.

I do some writing now called, "The SAND Room." SAND is an acronym for **S**earching **A**nd **N**oticing the **D**ivine. I believe through grief, we can be trained to notice things as never before, if we are willing to search through the rubble of our lives and find the diamond possibilities from the coal. God gives us so many gifts along the way. Those things are from GOD. They are not coincidences, or good luck, they are the Divine at work in our daily happenings. Even in the most tragic of circumstances, we can see God's mighty hand helping us, reaching out to us, and pulling us out of the devil's snares. God is not surprised at our difficulties, so why should we be surprised that our loving Father is there in the midst of them as our source of comfort and strength? Yes, He could take us right on out of here and onto Heaven if He wanted to, but He has a better purpose in mind. He wants that none should be lost. And if we are willing to be of service to our Father on this earth, sharing the Good News of Jesus Christ, our Savior, we can be a part of the team of bringing lost and hurting souls into His loving care. That is why we are still here. God is not trying to torture us. He is trying to teach us how to be a valuable servant in His Kingdom's work!

Maybe as I find the way out by going through it, I'll take them along with me, and they'll find the way out also—especially if someone has gotten stuck in the darkness.

I didn't know what the name of this book was going to be. Would it be, "Me, Myself, and The Great I AM?" Or, would it be, "Unending Grief" with the "Un" crossed out? I thought about many possibilities. And then I went to the Oakland Raiders' first preseason football game with my sister, Karen, a few weeks back. I was telling her about this project, and how it got started, and what God told me when I woke the next morning (This is explained in the Introduction). She said, "It Started in the Dark" sounds like the title to the book. Then she added, "And it ended in the light." Interesting. It was one of those light-bulb moments! I knew she was right about the title, and also about it ending in the light. Grief is so dark, and lonely, and hurting, and horrible, really. We can get stuck there in the dark. For some reason, it feels right to get stuck there. But it's not right! The Great I AM says He is the Great Healer. That includes us. God wants to heal our shattered hearts. He wants us to live fully again, and even thrive! We can trust God for that. And when we do, we will see it come to pass! I wouldn't be writing this book if that wasn't true. And if you need something to help you find your way out, I hope these writings will be a tool that you can use as a flashlight through your own dark night. The morning light **will** come. It will. Hang in there!

Maybe God knew I would not give up, no matter how much it hurt?

God knows what assignments to give each of His children. He also knows just what it will take to get our attention. I was a tough nut to crack! I don't like to even think that it took my child's Homegoing to reach the depths of my soul, but it did, and God knew that. I know that now. I think I might have always known that. When I was in my early twenties, I remember making a deal with God. I told Him, "You can do anything You want to me, God, but just don't paralyze me, or take my child." What was I saying? There must have been something in me that knew I could withstand most anything, just not one of those two things. Maybe I didn't want to need God, really? But He wanted me to need Him because He knew when I truly did, I would know that I needed nothing else. Not that I don't enjoy lots of other things, and love my husband, and family and friends as anyone does. But I know, if push comes to shove, I'm all God's. I'm all in! I'm sold out to Jesus! In that surrender, true freedom is found! And relationships can flourish. Isn't it strange how backward all the things of God seem on this earth, and yet they work so very well according to His plan in Heaven?

I know that it is possible, because I'm not the first
And I won't be the last, to feel all this hurt

So many have come before me and walked in very similar shoes. Who am I to write about all this and even think for a moment that I will come up with something new that might help another? I don't know. But I'm just trying to be obedient, and let it flow as God directs. Maybe it has been written about before, many times, but maybe for some reason you picked up this book and it will speak to you. Then, it will have been worth it. And honestly, I love to write, so no matter what happens, it is time well spent. God will use this book in whatever way He sees fit.

Gift #10 – None of what we are going through is useless. Our Father has a plan, and we're in it!

Have you seen, or are you looking for, the ways of God that those outside of your situation are not privy to?

Can you see any ways you can use the things you are learning now to help another in the future?

Record today's date and other notes you'd like to make:

The Great

<u>I AM</u>

For I know the plans I have for you," says the LORD. "They are plans for good and not for disaster, to give you a future and a hope.
Jeremiah 29:11 (NLT)

CHAPTER ELEVEN

Even when I walk through the darkest valley,
I will not be afraid for you are close beside me.
Psalm 23:4 (NLT)

<u>Me</u>

Chemotherapy

Tue, 18 Dec 2001

When Phil was first diagnosed, it changed our world; our whole life. He would have to undergo 9 months of intensive chemotherapy, followed by 2½ years of maintenance chemotherapy. Supposedly maintenance was easier than regular chemo, but we found as time went on, it built up in his system. What would wipe him out for a weekend in the beginning, ended up being close to a week later on.

Some say it takes 2-5 years to complete grief—whatever that means. Will it ever be really over? But I guess it's a return to a somewhat normal feeling inside. If that is true, then this journey resembles the other. We have just been diagnosed with "Grief."

The treatment plan will include maybe 9 months of intensive Grief, followed by 2½ years of maintenance Grief. At the end of that time, we should be finished, somewhat. That is a long battle! But we understand that, because of what Phil had to endure.

If our son could endure such a long haul, can't we? Don't we owe it to him to at least try and come out of this healthy? Should we be struggling with these feelings of giving up–of not wanting to go on–when we have only just begun the Grief treatment? I feel like a failure, that a young boy could do so well, and I can be such a wimp. What kind of a person am I? When it hurts a little, or even a lot, I want to call out, "STOP"! He never did that. All the times we packed up his bags to go to the hospital to make him "sick," even though he HATED it, he didn't fight us. He did what he had to do, without complaining. He went through all those years of suffering, and sickness, and being tired, and being weighted down with

Phil and I - Brunch at the top of the Bank America Building in San Francisco. (Age 11 in 1996)

exhaustion without complaining. How can I even think I have the right to complain now?

Thurs, 20 December 2001

We weep, and we grieve, and we miss him so, so much.

God knows that. God sees our tears; God may weep with us, as He must have done on the day His own Son died. The Father saw His Son's lifeless body as it hung on the Cross. He saw as it was buried in the tomb. He saw the shell that was left as the coldness that began to fill His physical body, the burial procedures, the weeping family, His mother, and His friends. But then He saw the resurrection of His Child **three days later**—*conquering death, and giving us all the Hope that we can cling to now.*

What joy that must have given God to finally say, "It is finished" from Heaven, also. It is finished. The sorrow will not last forever. The pain will pass away. The missing will be gone when we are reunited for eternity. What joy! The same joy we should feel deep inside. The joy that Christmas holds. The birth of our Savior. The Savior of the world. Come, all ye faithful, and He will give you rest.

I know that rest. I know what it is to be in it. And what it is to be out of it. What a difference Christ makes in our lives. What a difference He makes every day. But what a huge, spectacular, all-encompassing difference He makes when we need Him most— when we are so filled with sorrow that He is the only one who can lift us up out of the muck and mire. What a gift Jesus gives us every day when we open our hearts to all that He is doing to ease our burdens.

Sometimes I think it must take the lowest point in our lives, before we really open our eyes to Jesus and to really appreciate what He is offering us in the way of help, encouragement, and peace. To me, this year, the Prince of Peace means so much more than at any other time in my life. I need that peace above all else. Without *it, life is a tangled mess of feelings that tie into a knot of emotional destruction—one that twists and binds my insides until I think I can stand it no more. I look for Christ's peace. I crave His peace! And I find peace **only** with my Savior, and time spent with Him.*

<u>Myself</u>

Some say it takes 2-5 years to complete grief—whatever that means. Will it ever be really over?

I didn't want to be a "textbook" case. I wanted to move through grief quickly and easily. It wasn't happening. It took work, and it took time. The "experts" were right. It takes two to five years is about right. The first year, is the toughest. All the holidays and birthdays are tough. All the things that must be done for the first time are so difficult. The second year, the tears are less, but there are still many. It's not a whole lot easier, but somewhat. The third year, changes have usually taken place—babies may have been born, weddings may have been celebrated, perhaps there's been a move, or a new job. There are many things that show signs of "spring." The long winter "snow" starts to melt a little. The fourth year, better, but still the pain ebbs and flows, bringing tears and heartache. By the end of the fifth year, it seems it's time to release the pain, to let it go and move along—slowly at first, and then faster through each succeeding year. Life seems to be readjusting itself in a way that actually works somehow.

Should we be struggling with these feelings of giving up? Of not wanting to go on? When it hurts a little, or even a lot, I want to call out "STOP"!

When we hear of a couple that has been married, 50, 60, or sometimes even 70 years, and one spouse dies, many times we will hear of the other spouse leaving soon thereafter. Maybe God allows them to say, "I'm done here. Beam me up Scottie." I don't know, but it sure seems like it would be a relief in the early days of grief to just say, "Beam me up God. I'm done." It's a common emotion, and it can be worked through if we will just hang on and keep praying, and keep putting one foot in front of the other. Some give in to the temptation of suicide, and that doesn't help anyone. In fact, it hurts so many. Suicide is hard to understand for those left behind. My Grandma (not the one previously mentioned), took her own life. What I remember most from that decision is all the things that changed in the year following her death. There were so many things that had seemed hopeless to her, but she didn't stay on earth long enough to see how those situations would turn out. It was sad that she wasn't here to enjoy what happened in the following year. (It just dawned on me, Phil was even born that year.) We can't know what God is doing with our future, if we're not here to be a part of it.

God may weep with us, as He must have done on the day His own Son died.

My husband, Jim, says he understands the heartbreak of the Cross better because of watching his own son die. It does give us both a perspective on our Father sacrificing His only begotten Son on our behalf. It seems so wrong to see a child die. But I always tried to remind myself that the Father never asked us to do anything that He hadn't done, and even more. We loved on our son until his dying breath. Jesus was betrayed, abandoned, and tortured, willingly. The method our Father chose to rescue us, using His only Son, cannot be outdone on this earth with our own suffering, pain, and loss. Our pain is understood in Heaven's Throne Room.

What joy that must have given God to finally say, "It is finished" from Heaven, also. It is finished. The sorrow will not last forever. The pain will pass away.

The *Garden Mis-Adventure* with Adam and Eve has been reversed, and our relationship with our Father has been restored through Jesus Christ. All that took place so that we can grieve as those who DO HAVE HOPE. It had to feel WONDERFUL for Jesus to **know** what was being accomplished on the Cross that day, even if those who hung Jesus there didn't understand. Jesus said, "Father, forgive them, for they do not know what they are doing." Luke

23:34 (NIV) But one day, every knee will bow before our Lord. And those who have said, "Yes" to Jesus' saving grace will weep no more.

The Savior of the world. Come, all ye faithful, and He will give you rest. I know that rest, what it is to be in it, and what it is to be out of it.

To this day, I still practice what I learned early on in grief, finding rest in the peace offered to us from Heaven above. This world is a harsh place to live in, even for those living in the best this life has to offer. I once said if given the choice of a million dollars or peace, I would choose peace. There is nothing worse than not being at peace; nothing else compensates for unrest. We can't enjoy money, family, jobs, vacations, etc…if we are disturbed in our soul. We took a beautiful vacation to Hawaii when Phil

Diane and Phil in Hawaii, 2001   Jimm, Chris, Jim, and Phil

relapsed for the last time. We went to one of the most beautiful places on earth, experienced some of the most exciting adventures money can buy, stayed in luxurious places, and ate delicious food. To this day, I say it was one of the most blessed, most difficult vacations of my life. If each day there was not focused on the things of Jesus Christ and the Hope we have in Him, there was nothing there to be enjoyed. We were in paradise, because our son was very possibly soon leaving us for the real Paradise. Jesus had to give us rest in Him, so we could enjoy the rest of all He was offering us on this earth.

Sometimes I think it must take the lowest point in our lives, before we really open our eyes to Jesus and to really appreciate what He is offering us in the way of help, of encouragement, and of peace.

I wrote this early on. It was shortly before our first Christmas without Phil. He had only been gone just over a month. My eyes were like a little baby just out of the womb. I was crying, and unable to help myself, needing my Father's arms to hold me. I wasn't even near the lowest point yet, but it sure felt like it. It truly is a learning process that God takes us through, showing us that He is all the help we need. He teaches us how to use His help, when to apply it, and where, and then how to offer it to others. Just as a baby learns to roll over, to sit up, to crawl, and then to walk, etc… so we continue to mature as the born again children of God.

*I find that peace **only** with my Savior, and time spent with Him.*

This world offers us SO much! We can find great entertainment, beautiful scenery, powerful drugs, exotic drinks, and physical pleasures from rock climbing, to water skiing, to sex. There is music that can help our mind escape, and food that seems to satisfy our soul. For me, my oldest son's chocolate chip cookies are awesome. But NOTHING truly offers us what Jesus does. And He died to give it to us. This life is fleeting. It will all be gone one day, and the only thing ever-lasting is our Lord! How comforting it is to know that we have a solid foundation to live our lives on. Even here in the San Francisco Bay Area, where earthquakes are known to happen. Our whole house can shake, rattle, and roll into rubble, but our hearts can be strong because of what we have in Jesus! When we really begin to comprehend that one day we will live *happily ever after in Paradise*, we can learn to hang on to the end. Praise Jesus! He is what can keep us going longer than that little Energizer bunny ever will.

Gift #11 – The very worst in life can point us to the very best there is—Jesus!

Have you found that the hard times reveal that your only peace is in Jesus?

If not, are you willing to spend daily time in the Word and in prayer searching for His peace?

Record today's date and other notes you'd like to make:

The Great

<u>I AM</u>

Surely your goodness and unfailing love
will pursue me all the days of my life, and
I will live in the house of the LORD forever.
Psalm 23:6 (NLT)

CHAPTER TWELVE

So they hurried off and found Mary and Joseph, and the baby,
who was lying in the manger. When they had seen him, they
spread the word concerning what had been told them about
this child, and all who heard it were amazed at what
the shepherds said to them. But Mary treasured up
all these things and pondered them in her heart.
Luke 2:16-19 (NIV)

Me

Possibilities

Tuesday, 25 Dec 2001

Is it possible to have a joyful Christmas one day shy of six weeks
after your son dies? Is it possible to find peace on such a day? Is it
possible to experience some of the happiness from the past, before
your whole life had been changed, never to be the same again?
Yes. Yes it is! And I want you to know that. I want you to know that
even when the very worst thing possible happens—when your child
dies and there is nothing you want more for Christmas than to
have them back, and that is not possible—it is possible to rejoice. I

don't talk about something that I haven't experienced. I don't say this glibly, without emotion or feeling. I say this because I have experienced it. I have now lived through it, and as the day comes to a close, even I am still amazed at what an awesome God we have!

Why, oh why, do I still stand amazed at how much He loves us and wants to help us? I don't know. I guess because I'm still learning, and I will never know all that there is to know about our Lord until I, too, meet Him face to face. I wonder how Phil's first Christmas in Heaven was? How was the party? Was there one? Do they pick out a special day to celebrate Christ's earthly birth, or is every day "Christmas" in Heaven? I wouldn't be surprised. Why would they not celebrate the Lord every day when He is in their presence, as He should be in ours? But we get busy. We get busy working, playing, cleaning, shopping, or whatever, and Jesus is not our main focus. But in Heaven, how can He not be? There He is, right before their eyes. They can literally bow down at His feet and worship Him. Jesus can literally wrap His arms around them and comfort them, and share His wisdom. They know Jesus' "address," and He knows theirs. After all, Jesus did prepare a place for them, as He will for us. Ahhh...the wonder of Heaven.

I didn't know how I would do with Christmas. I started out pretty miserable to tell you the truth. Yesterday, Christmas Eve, I struggled as the day got started. I started with a heart ache the night before, then woke with a stomachache and then moved into a jaw ache. Some of the ways I grieve, I guess. I try to think of the heartache as a growing instead of a missing. Just like the Grinch, whose small heart "grew three sizes" that day, I think, that with all that I am feeling, my heart is growing and stretching and that is why it hurts so much. I try to think of my stomachache as a hunger for God. When it hurts I should go to His Word and eat and drink it in to fill the huge void. I still have not figured out what to do with the jaw ache, but I'm sure that will come in time. As the day went on, my misery would come and go as I would try different "tools" to help get through this time—like the Bible, praying, inspirational videos, and music. But actually, I thought it would be better to just get Christmas over with, and not have to think about it so much. Then God, who knows our every need, stopped by; not really God, but God's love through a faithful servant and friend of ours, Joan. She knocked on the door and dropped off a basket, and a card, then quickly left. I sat down and read the card, and it said that in the basket were four candles that Joan had saved from Phil's Memorial Service. (She provided 16 candles, one for each year of his life, the day of his service.) And there was a fifth candle in the basket also—a gold one; the others were white. The four white candles were to be lit by the four of us, in memory of Phil, and the gold candle was to be lit for all of them, all those lives that had been touched by Phil's. I set the basket on the dining room table and headed off to church, not knowing the impact that those candles would have and the peace God would bring into our home this Christmas.

When we arrived home from the Christmas Eve service, we sat down to some chili and cornbread, but not until I shared with Jim, Jimm, and Chris what the basket on the table was for. I read the card, and then we each unwrapped a thick white candle and set it before us on the table, along with the gold candle. We each lit a candle in Phil's memory and then I read, John 8:12 (NIV) as it was also written in the card. It reads: "When Jesus spoke again to the people, he said, 'I am the light of the world. Whoever follows me will never walk in darkness, but will have the light of life.'" We then joined hands as Jim prayed over our family, and our meal, thanking God for our many blessings, especially our extended family, friends, and the food provided. We ate in peace as we remembered Phil, and it was good.

The next morning, Christmas day, we repeated this once again, as we lit our candles, and read Scripture, and prayed before our meal. Later in the day, before we enjoyed our turkey dinner, we repeated it once again. In doing so, each time we honored our Savior, we gave thanks, and we remembered Phil and all that he meant to us.

I truly believe it will be one of our most memorable Christmases ever—not because of tears, or pain, or missing, but because of the peace that filled our home—because of the Savior, and Who He is and what He offers to us on His birthday. The greatest gifts ever— the gifts of peace, Hope, and eternal life. We sat there as a family mourning our loss and missing Phil, for sure, never doubt that, but also as a family with the Hope that one day we will all be together again, and the joy that brings. Phil is not dead; he is more alive than ever! And we are not dead because our grieving makes us feel that way; we are more alive than ever because, more than ever before, we feel the presence of the Lord as a family, and we see our need for a Savior.

*It's not dishonoring Phil to enjoy this day. It's in his honor and his memory that we enjoy this day, and keep him close, grieving as those **with** Hope. Praise God for His goodness. We see it so clearly.*

We thank you for all the prayers being said for our family, and for the protection and help they provided on this day, and every day.

Merry Christmas to all, and to all a good night!

Myself

Is it possible to experience some of the happiness from the past, before your whole life had been changed, never to be the same again?

Christmas day can either be one of the most blessed days of the year, or one of the loneliest. Holidays really bring things into the light, exposing them for what they are. While some are enjoying feasts and jolliness, some are truly not. This was a very, very, very difficult Christmas. It was ONLY the peace of Christ which gave us any way to endure what it seemed must be celebrated. We couldn't ignore Christmas—although I guess we could have. But then again, we would have missed so much; the special gift from a friend, the answered prayers being said by so many on our behalf, and the peace God was extending to our family if we would only just **believe**. We owed it to the pray-ers, to ourselves, and to our

God to "celebrate," even in our sadness. God's peace will guard our hearts and minds as we live in Christ Jesus. (Philippians 4:7)

I have now lived through it, and as the day comes to a close, even I am amazed still at what an awesome God we have!

We walked out that first Christmas, and many after it. And we now know, that with a focus on Jesus, each Christmas can get a little easier. As I may have mentioned earlier in these writings, our family went from "messed up" to "blessed up." From a very sad, grieving family of four, to a family of 12, including six

From Messed Up in 2001, to Blessed Up in 2013. What a difference in 12 years! God brought us two daughters-in-law and six grandchildren!!

grandchildren! We celebrate Christmas now with great joy, because of the healing that has come over time.

I didn't know how I would do. I started out pretty miserable to tell you the truth.

Our emotions really can cause physical aches and pains. I was experiencing that on that first Christmas Eve with Phil, and at other times in my life. When Phil was first going through Chemotherapy, I had a backache that grew increasingly worse. It got so bad I couldn't turn over at night without waking up from the pain. I thought I was surely sick, too, but I would have to deal with it later because I needed to focus on taking care of Phil then. What I realized was that it was simply stress. Those aches are red flags for me even today. When my shoulder blade starts to ache, or when my jaw starts hurting, it's time for me to slow down and get with God. Something is up, and I'm too stressed. I need to turn it around. Stressed spelled backwards is Desserts. That's much more enjoyable!

I think that with all that I am feeling my heart is growing and stretching and that is why it hurts so much.

As I read this again today, I really think it could be true. The heart is a muscle, and we can change our heart through physical exercise. But in 1Timothy 4:8 (NLT) it says, "Physical training is good, but training for godliness is much better, promising benefits in this life and in the life to come." I believe our heart really does grow stronger with Holy Spirit/Coach led training.

As the day went on, my misery would come and go as I would try different "tools" to help get through this time—like the Bible, praying, inspirational videos, and music.

We have to pull out all the stops to survive these times. There are many "tools" to use, and it is a good idea to get to know them. We have to learn when to stop, drop, and roll. When is it time to take a nap? Should we open up the Psalms and find some peace there?

Will a morning walk, with some good worship music playing, calm our nerves? How about even a funny movie? When I got off the phone with Phil's doctor one day, after she had just told me his cancer was back, we cried. Then we prayed, and then Phil said, "Let's watch a funny movie." So we did! Whatever it takes to get through, find it, and use it. God provides many good things for us—but alcohol, dangerous drugs, and things of that sort will only be setbacks, not steps forward.

Then God, who knows our every need, stopped by; not really God, but God's love through a faithful servant and friend of ours.

There is nothing like God using His people to help us in our time of need. I know it must have been difficult for Joan to deliver that gift to our home on Christmas Eve. That's not an easy assignment. It took courage, and it took following God even when it would have been easier not to. God knows our every need, and He will find people to help Him get His work done. I want to be that kind of person now. I want to be one who listens, obeys, and blesses others with God's loving suggestions on how best to do that.

"I am the light of the world. Whoever follows me will never walk in darkness, but will have the light of life." John 8:12 (NIV)

We **have** to "follow" Jesus through and out of our pain. Many times we would rather just stay in bed, and pull the covers over our head. Sometimes, maybe that's what we need to do. But if God is telling us to get up and go for a walk, we have to do it. If He is asking us to open up His Word, we need to do it. We have to "follow" Him out of the darkness. He is the only Light that will really help hurting hearts to recover. We can't do it on our own. Some have tried. Some seem like they have come through difficulties. But if we really sit and talk with them, and if they really are honest about what's going on, there is hemorrhaging from brokenness buried deep inside that was never healed through Jesus Christ. Guaranteed! I sat with a person one day, listening to many of her stories of the past. It appeared from the outside she had it all together. I found it wasn't true. I have never forgotten the hemorrhaging that was expressed on that day because Jesus Christ was not a part of her life. Instead of finding Jesus' healing power, there was hurt, and pain, and unforgiveness. She shared stories of misery, hopelessness, brokenness, resentment, etc… Only Jesus can cure such deep hurts. God designed us, He formed us, and only HE knows how to repair us. We have to put ourselves in His capable hands!

I truly believe, it will be one of our most memorable Christmas' ever—not because of tears, or pain, or missing, but because of the peace that filled our home.

We do all remember that Christmas, and have expressed how hard it was. But once again, like childbirth, we don't feel the pain anymore; we just remember it, and are grateful to have moved on from there. One thing we did on that first Christmas was give Phil's brothers, Jimm and Chris, a gift from Phil. With some of Phil's insurance money, we bought one year of Oakland Raiders season tickets. We put a gift certificate in a Raiders' glass mug at their place setting. We told them they could choose to sit in the stadium wherever they wanted. That was twelve years ago, and they still have those two seats. Jimm has since moved to Oregon, so Chris usually goes with a friend. Jimm joins him once a year for a game. And as I just wrote, my sister, Karen, and I went to the first preseason game this year because Chris was out of town. It was the first time I had ever used the tickets, and it was very special. Although, they did pick the "Black Hole" seating area, which is a pretty crazy place to be. But we had a great time! We continue to remember Phil in so many ways.

Phil is not dead; he is more alive than ever! And we are not dead because our grieving makes us feel that way; we are more alive than ever because more than ever before, we feel the presence of the Lord as a family and we see our need for a Savior.

It is imperative to understand that our loved ones are more alive than ever! Their earthly bodies have died; their spirit and soul have not. They live on, in a much better place if they were believers in

Jesus Christ. And only God truly knows a heart on the last day on this earth. So we can hold onto the hope that they came to know Jesus before they took their last breath. God does not let His creations die without giving us every opportunity to know Him and become His children. And even though something inside of us *seemingly* died when our loved ones left us, it is not truly dead. We can live fully again one day with Jesus as our Hope! Jesus can resurrect our lives out of the rubble, because He was resurrected from the dead. We have to give it a great deal of time, and a great deal of prayer. But we will rise again!! When we see our need for a Savior, we are absolutely looking in the **right** direction. Once again, guaranteed! Been there. Done that! Don't need a t-shirt! It can be written on our hearts, in our minds, and worn on our faces! I wrote a long time ago, "If Jesus doesn't work, I'll be the first one to tell you." I found out He does work. I'm here to tell you!

We thank you for all the prayers being said for our family.

We can't really know the full power of prayers being said on our behalf, but I shudder to think what this all would have been like without prayer. So many think about the grieving on those difficult days, and are faithful to pray. They don't have to be complicated, formal, *thee* and *thou* prayers; just heartfelt calls out to God to help someone who is in need. God will hear, and He will send what is needed to get us through our most difficult times. Let's be faithful to pray for one another. We may think we don't see all that prayers accomplish—but then again, I'm sitting here writing all this today as a result of those prayers. So the words you're reading might be a good visual from which to draw strength. I can truly say, "God is good." And I can truly say, "God is a healing God" because He healed my heart. There was a day when I had my doubts about God's healing power. After all, we prayed for Phil, and he is no longer here with us. But today I know God has a perfect plan. Some live short lives, some long ones. But God will always heal a heart surrendered to Him. Glory be to God!

Gift #12 – Realizing a need for a Savior, and finding He is with us, and He works!

What has been your most difficult day, and how did you get through it?

What God-given tools have been most useful for you?

Record today's date and other notes you'd like to make:

The Great

<u>I AM</u>

*You will know at last that I, the Lord,
am your Savior and your Redeemer,
the Mighty One of Israel.*
Isaiah 60:16 (NLT)

CHAPTER THIRTEEN

God, for whom and through whom everything was made, chose to bring many children into glory. And it was only right that he should make Jesus, through his suffering, a perfect leader, fit to bring them into their salvation.
Hebrews 2:10 (NLT)

Me

The New Year

Tue, 01 Jan 2002

Phil didn't have to get up this morning. He was already up. He didn't have to ring in the New Year, for there are no new years in Heaven. Time is not relevant in eternity. How can a human mind fathom that thought? No beginning, no end, forever and forever... I find it hard sometimes. I try to picture Phil in Heaven, with God, with Jesus Christ, actually living there and having everything he will ever need or want. He took nothing with him but himself. He faced God by himself, no Mom or Dad standing there beside him. He stood alone before the Throne of God, complete in who he was —answering for himself for the first time. He never had to do that

*on earth, because he was still a child. He never had to experience
some of the other difficult parts of life like getting a job, figuring
out what he wanted to be and moving toward that goal, meeting a
wife, having children, and all the decisions and responsibilities
that would entail. Phil talked to me about those things and never
having to deal with that. He was kind of glad. I was kind of glad
for him. I told him that he would go right from us taking care of
him, to God taking care of him. He didn't have much of a problem
with that.*

*My brother, Rick, tells me of a song that is out right now
expressing that very thing. How awesome it will be to finally be in
God's presence and finally see for ourselves all that we have
believed in, having not seen, but finally being there. I try to
imagine that about Phil. I cling to that thought, asking God to help
me see it, and realize it, and know that Phil is content, happy, and
well taken care of. As a mother, it's so hard to release that
responsibility of caring for him—to actually **let go** and know that
my job is finished concerning his care. Maybe that is why it is so
hard to lose a child; to let them go? Because when they are placed
in our arms, crying, naked, and totally dependent on us, we take
them into our hearts. We give them all our love, and we protect
them with every ounce of energy we have, not wanting anything
bad to happen to them. And then suddenly, that job is finished?
They are in God's arms, out of our reach, and we are no longer
responsible? How do we adjust to that thought? Not easily, I can
tell you. My greatest need is to know that Phil is okay. For some
reason, I have to keep asking God to help me with that, to remind
me that he doesn't need me anymore. I don't know if that is the
struggle every mom has when they lose their child, but it is one of
mine. How can my job be finished so quickly? Like Phil's questions
about the simplicity of getting into Heaven. He asked, "Isn't there
something I need to do? It just seems too simple." And we
discussed God's gift, and God's grace. I now have the same
question. Isn't there something I need to do? Can I simply release
my child into God's Heavenly arms and go on with my life,
knowing he is fine? There is such a vacancy left behind by giving
up that responsibility. There is such a missing, and a longing, and
a need to nurture. I dream about the day Phil and I will be*

reunited—when we can hug each other and stand face to face, laughing and talking of all that we have experienced here on earth, and how good and true God's Word is. I long for the day when Phil might say to me, "You were so right, Mom. Thank you for helping me know that God is all that He says He is. Thank you for encouraging me when I was most scared, when I longed to go Home to Heaven, but wanted so badly to stay with you. Thank you for letting me go, knowing I would soon feel better and for loving me enough to do that for me willingly." I know we will rejoice together on that day, and I look forward to it with great anticipation!

I need to remember that when I want to crawl into a hole and have a pity party. Not only that, but the fact that when Jesus left this earth, our Heavenly Father sent the Holy Spirit to indwell in every believer, as a Helper. God did not leave us alone, abandoned to face these trials alone. Jesus paved the way to Heaven by dying on the Cross—then He left us with all the Help we'll ever need to survive until that day comes.

Happy New Year!
The Shores

Myself

He didn't have to ring in the New Year, for there are no new years in Heaven. Time is not relevant in eternity.

Many say there is no time in Heaven, but in Revelation 8:1 (NIV) it says, "When he opened the seventh seal, there was silence in heaven for about half an hour." This seems to indicate there is time in Heaven. I wasn't familiar with this Scripture when I wrote this 12 years ago. I don't know how it works, and I still can't imagine no beginning and no ending. But I can imagine that time really doesn't matter all that much. With all of eternity to live in Heaven, our lives here are just such a blip in comparison. I have had to remember that when a day seemed like forever.

He stood alone before the Throne of God, complete in who he was.

We would like to hold our child's hand right into the Throne Room and make the introductions. It seems we should be able to. After all, they are just children. But it isn't necessary. No one loves them more than our Heavenly Father. No one will care for them better than He does, can, and will. Phil's relationship with Jesus, at the age of 16, was his, and his alone. Our job, on this side of Heaven, is to share God's love with everyone we know. To share Him with our children, grandchildren, friends, family, and even strangers. We can rest in what happens in Heaven, and continue to do what we are called to do here.

I told him that he would go right from us taking care of him, to God taking care of him.

Talking about what was to come was done out of respect for Phil. It was not done to be morbid or hopeless. I read once that we pay no respect to those dying if we will not discuss it with them. They know they could be dying, we know they could be dying, and to not talk about it robs them, and us, of what is needed. These are not easy conversations to have, but they are priceless.

There is a place on a road here, in the Bay Area, that always takes me back to a statement made by Phil about a month before he went Home. Do you have those places that always remind you of certain conversations? Every time I drive down that road, and make that curve to the right, I remember Phil saying, "If I'm this happy here, just think how happy I will be in Heaven." I marvel at that statement, coming out of a boy who had fought cancer for 5 ½ years, and was very sick. And I cherish that memory. If we had not talked openly about what was happening, and what could happen, and where eternity would be spent, we would not have those conversational gifts to hold onto still today!

As a mother, it's so hard to release that responsibility of caring for him. To actually let go and know that my job is finished concerning his care. How do we adjust to that thought?

The reality of the situation does not instantly absorb into our thought process. Jim and I had gone to the mortuary with our Pastor, Dave. We walked through the room full of caskets, needing to make a decision. We made our way into the office to discuss our plans, and suddenly I started to cry. Very normal, you might be thinking. But what was mind-blowing to me was the real reason I had started to cry. I turned to Pastor Dave and tearfully said, "I was just thinking, we need to hurry up. I need to get home and take care of Phil."

My greatest need is to know that Phil is okay.

When I read this today, it is eye-opening for me. I don't remember this being my greatest need, but if I wrote it at the time, then it must have been true for me then. As the years have gone on, I truly **do know** that Phil is okay. I have studied Heaven, and I think about Heaven, a lot! I know the Father's love for us more then ever before, and I know that Phil doesn't need me or anything else on this earth now. He is fully provided for. That *knowing* definitely took time—time with God in prayer, and being in the Word.

I now have the same question. Isn't there something I need to do?

I understand this is a great struggle, obviously, because I certainly struggled with it. I just talked with a mom the other night, one who I know has a daughter in Heaven. In our very brief conversation, she said, "It's just so hard to let them go." Yes, it is!! It seems wrong. It seems disrespectful. It takes work and trust in who God says He is. It was good to hear that she was starting to make it through after five years. Five years does seem to mark a new beginning into the rest of our lives.

Can I simply release my child into God's Heavenly arms and go on with my life, knowing he is fine?

I have had many torturous thoughts through the years about the things I should have done or said differently with Phil. But I always have to keep coming back to the truth: IT DOESN'T

MATTER NOW!! I know that Phil is not in Heaven wishing I had been a better Mom. I know that he is not waiting for me to get there so we can discuss all the mistakes I made in his life. I know that when we are in Heaven together, the love is so pure and the forgiveness is so complete, none of our mistakes here in our relationships will matter any more. If I'm living in my past mistakes while here, I'm giving in to the enemy and his crafty ways. I have had to learn NOT to do that. It is hard, and it takes work, but it is worth it!

I dream about the day Phil and I will be reunited.

I know we should be thinking about meeting Jesus, and I have to admit, maybe my priorities are off. But when I think about Heaven, I think about seeing Phil. I'm still working on this one. Maybe it's just that I can talk to God every day, but I don't get to talk to Phil every day. In fact, the Bible is clear that we are not to try to communicate with the dead. So, I don't talk to Phil. Oh, sometimes I talk to his picture hanging on the wall, but that's hopefully not the same as trying to communicate with him in Heaven. If I want to get a message to Phil, I ask God to pass it along to him—to tell him I love him, and I miss him. Many have asked me if I sense his presence with me? Honestly, I don't. Once, during a baptism where Phil was being mentioned, and the impact he had had on this man's life, I had a sense that maybe he was witnessing this event; but that's about it. I sense God's presence, not Phil's.

"Thank you for letting me go, knowing I would soon feel better and for loving me enough to do that for me willingly."

I know beyond a shadow of a doubt that the Holy Spirit was in charge on this one. How does a mother tell her child it is okay to go Home? The Holy Spirit was speaking through me, especially during those final minutes of Phil's life on earth. I encouraged him to go, that his job was finished. I don't understand that myself, so if you question my sanity, I can understand that. I know I was in "encouragement" mode. I even told a friend today that I stayed strong for Phil right up to the end, doing what he needed done. But the minute he was gone, I knew I was a "goner." I was going to grieve, and grieve hard now! I don't know that that was kind to my other two boys, ages 20 and 23 at the time. But I was probably exhausted. And somehow I knew, if I didn't take care of myself, I wouldn't be able to be there for them in the future. I had nothing left to give at that point, and I knew it. Twelve years later, I still know when I need to retreat, but it's not a bad thing. It is a time of drawing close to God, understanding that we have to give out of His excess. When our Lord fills us up with His love and compassion, it can then overflow onto others. Without being attached to the Vine, as branches, we wither and die. It makes me think of a plant out back, that I forget to water. It starts to droop, and just a bit of water perks it right up. Our spiritual lives must be very much like that; when we droop, it's only God's Living Water that can truly revive us!

I need to remember that when I want to crawl into a hole and have a pity party.

The hole is big, and it is deep, and it is tempting! We all go there in the beginning. And while there, we fill that hole with our tears. But we can't stay there, or we will drown in that pit. As the years go on, we should be able to visit that pit less and less, until eventually we can avoid it almost all the time. Just in the last week I have been with two Moms who have children in Heaven, one I mentioned previously. Both of them are starting to come alive again, realizing that life goes on. They are starting to not only look like they are surviving such a tremendous loss, but they are starting to thrive again! Both of them love Jesus. Both of them held onto their faith even when they didn't understand, through the anger, and through the tremendous pain. Yes, they questioned, and argued, and felt it was unfair. That's okay. God can take it. He is bigger than it all. And God will see us through if we will stick with Him!! Don't let go of God's hand. He knows the way out!

Not only that, when Jesus left this earth, He sent the Holy Spirit to indwell in every believer, as a Helper. God did not leave us alone.

God is SO smart. He knows how much we need Him. I can't imagine living in pre-Jesus days, when the Holy Spirit would just visit in certain people, coming and going. We are truly gifted today, as believers, to have His indwelling Spirit with us constantly. We are sealed when we believe in what Jesus died to give us. It says in Hebrews 2:15 (NLT) that Jesus delivered "...those who have lived all their lives as slaves to the fear of dying." We don't need to fear death anymore. And we don't need to fear for our loved ones who have died and live in Heaven. They are not alone. We are not alone. And we can all rejoice in the wonderful eternity together planned for all who will believe in Jesus as their Savior!! What better plan could there be than the one devised by our loving Father. It is perfect! Death seems cruel, but actually living here on this earth for all of eternity, with all this pain and suffering, would be the cruelest thing of all. Death is God's way out for us. It is a gift that He gives to all of us when our job is finished, at whatever age that comes. No one is going to live forever on this earth in its present condition. Praise Jesus!

Gift #13 – Knowing that Jesus has provided exactly what we all need!

Who or what is it that you have not been able to let go of?

What keeps you holding on? As you trust in God, are you willing to start releasing your grip a little bit more each day?

Record today's date and other notes you'd like to make:

The Great

I AM

Because God's children are human beings—made of flesh and blood—the Son also became flesh and blood. For only as a human being could he die, and only by dying could he break the power of the devil, who had the power of death. Only in this way could he set free all who have lived their lives as slaves to the fear of dying.
Hebrews 2:14-15 (NLT)

CHAPTER FOURTEEN

Greater love has no one than this, that he
lay down his life for his friends.
John 15:13 (NIV)

Me

Willing

Tue, 08 Jan 2002

I was just listening to a song in the car that said, "...to be willing to die, so that another may live." It started the tears flowing as I wondered if Phil had to die so that another might live? Was that the reason for his death, to show another the way? I know that Jesus died so that others may live, but do you realize that Phil was willing to do that for you?

The song went on to say, "...there is no greater love than this." Where would a young boy acquire that kind of love for another, if not from God?

Phil's death did not pave the way to Heaven for you, Christ's did. And Phil's death was not the perfect sacrifice, because he was a sinner, like all the rest of us. Christ was the only One who ever died a sinless death, thereby becoming the perfect sacrifice. But Phil's death was a sacrifice, I believe. Why else would God have called him Home at such a young age? And you know what? Phil understood this, and was willing to give up his own life to show others the way. He said as much. When Phil was baptized on April 14, 2001, my sister Karen was singing some songs and saying a few words, and one of the things she did was to have Phil step up in front of everyone for a few moments. She then asked the crowd of approximately 75 friends and relatives who had gathered to witness this event, if anyone there had been affected by Phil's life, or grown in their faith because of Phil? Almost everyone there raised their hand as Phil looked over this "cloud of witnesses."

Therefore, since we are surrounded by such a great cloud of witnesses, let us throw off everything that hinders and the sin that so easily entangles, and let us run with perseverance the race marked out for us. Hebrews 12:1(NIV)

Some time later, Phil and I were talking about why he was going through this trial, and he brought up that moment at his baptism. He said, "Maybe that was why?" How could a young boy possibly fathom the reasoning of God to use his life with this trial, so that others might know God better? Not only that, he was willing to accept this trial, this responsibility given to him, as a light in this world—and without anger. Here he was, 15½ years old, in front of this crowd of witnesses, about to be baptized in the name of Jesus Christ, confessing his faith in a God who had allowed him to endure years of treatments, years of tiredness, and years of wondering if he would live or die from this disease. He was still willing to confess his love for God the Father, and be baptized in the name of His Son, Jesus, because that was where his Hope was. That was where his peace was, and where his answers were. Maybe not all the answers while still in this world, but definitely in the next. Phil was a young man, willing to lay down his life for others, to maybe show them the way. How do you refuse that kind of faith? That kind of devotion to God? And if you do, my heart hurts even deeper than in the loss of my precious son. In the stubbornness of human nature, some would choose to not even find out if this is the truth, but simply rule it out because their pride may keep them from examining it before rejecting it.

Those who love us, who love our family, who watched Phil grow from childhood into being a teenager, and watched Phil suffer and endure this disease for some unknown reason, I would think they would like to get to the bottom of why that might be. We live without Phil's presence now. We must wait to see him on the other side, and simply be satisfied with our memories of our sweet son, and my heart aches to think that his life might have been wasted on some. If some consider all that God offers, and truly open their hearts to His calling, and then still refuse Him, that would be one thing, because we are given that free choice. But to not even look in that direction in honor of Phil's memory and out of respect for him, makes losing him even more painful. Phil was willing to die so that you might see Heaven one day. He really was! He accepted that job given to him. Can you accept the responsibility of watching that happen and give God a chance to use him in that way?

Yesterday I thought about Phil never walking through our front door again; never going into his room to sleep in his bed, put on the glasses that sit on his dresser, or use the remote that still sits on his nightstand. He could walk right back into our lives with hardly missing a step. Our world is still set up for him. He might notice that his dog has a new collar, or that I have a few more gray hairs, but other than that, this would still be his place in the world. But he will not be doing that. Then God helped me see it another way. Phil will never walk in our front door again, but he WILL greet me as I walk through the gates of Heaven. He will be there to welcome me Home to Heaven, and show me the place that has been prepared for me. I hope he can welcome you, too, along with all your other friends and relatives that have gone ahead of you. I hope they will be there waiting for you. But if not, you could be the first to be there waiting for the ones who come behind you. There will be no greater joy than that, just as there is no greater love than one who will lay down his life for us.

My son is gone from this earth. But he died for a reason, and that reason may be you! Christ died also, and rose three days later, to make the way for all of us. If you had been the only person on earth, Jesus would have done that just for you, because He loves you that much. At least consider it. It can do you no harm. But it can do you an eternity of good!

I will miss Phil every day I live on this earth. This morning as I was driving to Bible Study, I thought about living one more day, growing one day older, and one day closer to seeing Phil again. It doesn't mean I won't enjoy the life I have left here to live, but I will live every day with one foot on this earth, and one foot in Heaven —never viewing this world the same again, and never viewing Heaven the same way again.

Is what I write to you being bold? You bet it is! Am I totally comfortable with it? No! But I want to share the good, the bad, and the ugly with you. Phil's life deserves that much. This world offers me a lot, but it doesn't offer me the one thing I am missing most right now, my son. Only God offers that to me, and I gladly accept Jesus' offer to see my son again. What a glorious day that will be! That is Good News!

Love, Diane

Myself

It started the tears flowing as I wondered if Phil had to die so that another might live? Was that the reason for his death, to show another the way?

Of course we look for the reasons why things happen. Sometimes we get some answers; many times we don't. It's not wrong to wonder why and to ask God about it. But we shouldn't get stuck there when the answers don't come. A friend, Karen, gave us a book when Phil was first diagnosed. It said, instead of asking, "Why me?" Ask, "What now?" That was very simple, but very good advice. So many would say, "I don't know how you do it.

How do you handle all that it entails when your child has cancer?" There really isn't a question of how, there really isn't a choice. You do it because it is the assignment you have been given during this season of life.

Phil and I were talking about why he was going through this trial, and he brought up that moment at his baptism. He said, "Maybe that was why?"

My sister asking that question at Phil's baptism was really a gift to him. It gave him a visual to think about, and draw some comfort from. He needed that. We needed that! Our lives here are so short. If they can be used to help another, what better purpose can we have? When our eternity is secured through Jesus Christ, the only thing really to follow that up with is to help others find Him also. That is why I write to this day!

Phil was a young man, willing to lay down his life for others, to maybe show them the way. If some consider all that God offers, and truly open their hearts to His calling, and then still refuse Him, that would be one thing, because we are given that free choice. But to not even look in that direction in honor of Phil's memory and out of respect for him, makes losing him even more painful.

We want our loved ones lives to count for something. If it seems there is no reason for the suffering, and the loss, then it makes it just that much harder. We are here to help one another, to share our stories, our experiences, and the lessons learned, and pass them on. I sat with a woman yesterday going through some difficulties. She is just enough younger than me, for me to have already walked through much of what she was talking about. It felt very much like the verse in Titus 2:4 (NLT), "These older women must train the younger women to love their husbands and their children..." This world can still work as God designed it in many ways. One of which, is to help each other along by sharing our lives with each other.

He could walk right back into our lives with hardly missing a step. Our world is still set up for him.

Interesting... I think about this now, in our present living situation. I wonder where Phil would fit in, where he would be living, etc...? So much has changed that the constant reminders of coming across things that were his, or doing things without him, has changed quite a bit. Most of the firsts have been gone through, and the seconds, and the thirds. We have learned how to live without his presence. There isn't a forgetting in that, but an acceptance. There isn't a lack of love in that, but a Greater Love that has comforted our hearts. And it is good, because God is so very good!

Phil will never walk in our front door again, but he WILL greet me as I walk through the gates of Heaven. It doesn't mean I won't enjoy the life I have left here to live, but I will live every day with one foot on this earth, and one foot in Heaven.

I have voiced this to many people, about living with one foot on earth, and one foot in Heaven each day. It is a huge BLESSING to have someone we dearly love living in Heaven. It makes Heaven so important, and takes our focus off just this earth. The "luxury" of not thinking about our eternal lives is no longer a possibility, and we are glad. I am GLAD! Going Home is looked forward to. I understand why it says in Matthew 5:4 (NIV), "Blessed are those who mourn, for they will be comforted." There is a comfort found in mourning. When our focus is more and more on Jesus, and less and less on the things of this earth, it is as it should be. That is how God designed us. It makes everything here less important, and more precious at the same time. We know we can't hold onto things, people, or whatever we have here, as tightly, because they are not ours. The Lord gives and takes away. And blessed be the Name of the Lord! It took a long time before I could sing those words again. But it is possible now, and it is okay now, and I pray one day it will be okay for you, too.

Is what I write to you being bold?

I wonder, was I more passionate deep in my grief? Or am I more passionate now about the things of God? I know back then I was fighting for my son. I wanted what he endured to count for something. And I don't know to this day how many lives were changed, or continue to be changed, because he lived. But I do know one life that will **never** be the same, and that is mine! And I am thankful that Phil lived. He was not a planned child. He was a total surprise. Our other two boys were part of "our" plan, Phil was not. I know now he was a gift from God. I wondered when Phil got sick, "Why him, Lord?" I could understand if one of our other two boys got sick, and why God would have given us a third child. But why was God taking the child that was totally His plan from the beginning? Maybe Phil's life and death made me bolder for God? Actually, there is no maybe about it. This once painfully shy girl/woman has been changed. Speaking in front of others is not one of my top fears anymore. Living to please others more than God is not a huge temptation for me now. I see Phil's life as a perfectly planned out sixteen years. I don't have to like what has happened, but I have learned to have a peace about what God is doing with and through it all.

Gift #14 – Beginning to see the intricate ways God is working when times are tough!

Are you actively looking for God in the midst of what hurts so much?

Have you seen even just small slivers of what good this can bring to God's Kingdom work?

Record today's date and other notes you'd like to make:

The Great

I AM

He said to them, "Go into all the world and preach the good news to all creation."
Mark 16:15 (NIV)

CHAPTER FIFTEEN

*Now is your time of grief, but I will see you again
and you will rejoice, and no one will take away your joy.*
John 16:22 (NIV)

Me

Helpful Gestures

Sat, 12 Jan 2002

*Have you ever wondered what helps a grieving person the most?
Have you wondered what words to say? What words to write?
What cards to send? What gestures would mean the most? I don't
really have any perfect or complete answers to those questions,
because each day is different, each person is different and each
situation surrounding a loss is different. But I want to share one
gesture with you, just to let you know how much little things can
mean a lot—how they can change a morning of grief into a
morning of joy, and how the person who did it may never realize
what happened when they took a few moments to reach out and
touch another person. Here is my experience for today...*

My heart was heavy this morning. I was bit exhausted once again from another week gone by. I relish my time with God—my time reading His Word and the peace that comes from that. I continue to look for God throughout my day; looking for things that will lighten my heart. I wonder what direction He will take me, and how He will help me get through this missing, and enjoy the day ahead? I clicked on an e-mail message from a friend and found a passage of Scripture that had been included in that e-mail. It seemed to be just what I needed, so I turned to that section in the Bible and started reading John 16:22 (NIV), "Now is your time of grief, but I will see you again and you will rejoice, and no one will take away your joy." Right above that in verse 21 it says: "A woman giving birth to a child has pain because her time has come; but when her baby is born she forgets the anguish because of her joy that a child is born into the world."

We mothers can relate to that, because if we didn't forget the "anguish," we would NEVER have another child! Never ask a mother who has just delivered if she would like more children. Wait at least a day or so! It doesn't take long. We are so much in love with that baby; of course we would go through it again. The only problem then is wondering how we could ever love another child as much as we love the first one? That problem is solved when the next baby is born. Love at first sight!

And so my thoughts went this morning—thinking about the anguish, and the pain, and the joy that will follow it. I read through this section, about Jesus' last moments on this earth with His disciples. He was trying to explain to them that He would be going away, and they will mourn, but after a little while they will see Him again and their grief will turn to joy. He was telling them these things so that they would have peace. He was the Prince of Peace. When He appeared to the disciples after His resurrection, the first thing He said was, "Peace be with you!" Again He said, "Peace be with you!" Without peace, there is no joy, there is no fun, there is no pleasure—there are simply anxious thoughts, stomachaches, stress, and tears. I need the peace of God like never before, because at this time in my life, there is no in between. I am either in God's peace, or I am a mess! And I can go from one to *the other without warning. I think that is what grief is. Emotions can get out of control, and mine are only controlled at all by the peace of God which transcends understanding. I am able to feel that kind of peace. But with fresh grief, it is a constant process of staying focused and asking God for help. And because it is a constant work in progress, the small gestures of others are what sometimes keep me focused. When I find myself in a fog, not knowing which way to turn, and someone sends me a message, a verse, a card, or gives me a hug with a warm smile that shows me they care, or tells me about a song that I then listen to, or shares an encouraging word etc... Sometimes those things are all I need to make it through those next few hours. Sometimes they think they are not helping, or there must be something more they can do; it is such a small thing, after all. But it **is** the small things that add into the big things that carry me from hour to hour, and from day to day.*

*It's just like my questions to God. A lot of them are small requests. And usually they are repeated day after day, sometimes in the same day. Requests like, "Help me! Give me strength. Let me know that Phil is okay without me." Many different things, but things I repeat over and over until I move onto another phase of recovery —small things, one step at a time—nothing huge, just reassurances. And your gestures **are** part of that whole process.*

When Phil was sick, I learned to use "tools" to cope: inspirational books, prayers, the Bible, CD's, writing, fun times, quiet times, time with Phil, time away. A little bit of this, a little bit of that, but things that helped me get through each day. This time of grief is no different. It will be years of a little bit of this and a little bit of that, until it all adds into healing from the greatest pain I have ever felt. And I guess what I am trying to say here is, don't think that because you have not painted a Picasso and given it to me to show you care, or you have not flown me to Tahiti for a vacation getaway, that you are not helping me. You help me by just showing that you care, in all the little things along the way. It takes a community of caring people to help a grieving person recover. Each person in that community does one small part here and there to keep us moving forward, one inch at a time, until those inches turn into feet and those feet turn into miles. And years down the road we are able to look back and see how far we have come. When the recovery is measured in inches in the beginning, it seems like a long road ahead and we need all the encouragement we can get, a little bit at a time. Never think it is unneeded or too small to be noticed. I have noticed them all, believe me, and I thank God for all the kind gestures we have been shown along the way. You may never know when you have just turned my mourning into joy because you have done something that shows me a new and different way to look at the trial I am going through. You may never know, but I do, and God does. I hope if I do not thank you all personally, you will still feel the joy in your heart that you have given to me.

For today, John 16:22 carried me through this morning. I will grieve for awhile, but my grief WILL turn to joy. My anguish will be forgotten when I see Phil again. I was reminded of that in God's Word this morning, because Graham took the time to share it with me. It was a small gesture that transformed my day. A blessing from a friend who showed he cared, as so many of you have also done. Thank you.

Love, Diane

Myself

Have you ever wondered what helps a grieving person most?

It still amazes me that I wrote things that I was going through, and how I thought it was going to help me, and it actually did. All those little gestures, and tools, and everything else God gives to us along the way really do work. What I felt at that time were little bits of relief from the pain. Many years later, all those bits are the pieces that expand into a healed heart. Maybe we think that when tears still fall occasionally, it means healing hasn't taken place. I think we wouldn't be human if tears didn't still fall 10, 20, even 30 years later. Even the large scar I got at the age of two from an accident is still evident; I can still see it, and feel it. But it doesn't define me, and make me cry out, "Why God? Why?" It only reminds me that I am human, and that God heals in miraculous ways.

I clicked on an e-mail message from a friend and found a passage of Scripture that had been included in that e-mail. It seemed to be just what I needed.

God knows what we need each given day. He uses His people to share when we are lost in the darkness not knowing which way to turn. Just this morning I felt a nudge from God to post something on Facebook about who God is. I don't know whose heart it will touch today, but I know that I have to be faithful to obey those nudges so as not to miss helping someone with their little "bit" that is needed today. So many helped me, and I hope and pray they are helping you too.

I need the peace of God like never before, because at this time in my life, there is no in between. I am either in God's peace, or I am a mess!

It's said, "Desperate times call for desperate measures." There is no more desperate time than losing a loved one, whether that comes with death, divorce, or separation. When we are missing someone, and our circumstances have changed drastically because of it, we NEED God like never before! If we don't search for God in the missing, we will search for what is unhealthy for us, guaranteed. How do I know that? Because, if we are filling our need with anything other than God, we are using the wrong remedy for what He has brought into our lives for a reason. We can argue against this, and use other things as a substitute, but we are only delaying and/or missing the lessons needed altogether. It is our choice. Philippians 4:6 says we aren't to worry about anything; instead we are to pray about everything. Most times we end up worrying about everything, and praying about very little. For some strange reason, we think this works better. I know, I find myself doing the same. But worrying doesn't work, and God **does** work. So let's "do the math" there!

And because it is a constant work in progress, the small gestures of others are what sometimes keep me focused. But it's the small things that add into the big things that carry me from hour to hour, and from day to day.

Work is the key word here. Grief is HARD WORK! We'd like to get out of it, take a long lunch break, or an even longer vacation. But there is no getting away from it. So, we have to work at grief to get through it. No one can carry us through our grief, except for our Father in Heaven through the Hope of His Son. God can carry us if we curl up into His arms and let Him. If we fight Him, run away from Him, and ignore Him, we are delaying what He wants to do for us. We all have days like this, granted, but let's not let them rule our lives. Let's let God rule our lives, and He will bring us through what hurts most!

When Phil was sick, I learned to use "tools" to cope.

A techie has his tools, so does a plumber, and even a hairstylist. I should know. I am one! I always carry my tools in my trunk because I never know when I will need them. My husband always has at least his multi-tool on his belt. He uses it all the time. He needs it even on Christmas morning for the grandkids' new toys. For safety measures, sometimes it seems that they are locked in a vault! God, too, gives us His tools to use. He shares them with us. He is most generous. God also teaches us how to use them. They can be foreign to us in the beginning. Our Bibles can seem stiff, and unfamiliar. I used to read a lot of Max Lucado books. Max's books helped me understand the Bible better. I didn't know a lot of worship songs, but I got to know them, and I found my favorites that I used to help me focus on better things. I used worship songs in the car, and on my walks. We have to use what God gives us along the way.

It will be years of a little bit of this and a little bit of that, until it all adds into healing from the greatest pain I have ever felt. I guess what I am trying to say here is, don't think that because you have not painted a Picasso and given it to me to show you care, or you

*have not flown me to Tahiti for a vacation getaway, that you are
not helping me.*

I'm guilty of it too, thinking what I'm doing might not be a big
help. But it all helps, and it's all needed. Sometimes in our lives,
we are on the side of needing, sometimes we are on the side of
giving. My Aunt Margie *did* help us get to Hawaii, when needed,
as did our Pastor John. (Not Tahiti, but close!) There are so many
reminders now, not of our loss, but of the goodness shown to us
through the years. God's love pours into our lives through others.

*And years down the road we are able to look back and see how far
we have come.*

This is truer than I ever thought possible, really. Looking back is
much easier than looking forward. But, we have to move forward,
to be able to look back. I was just talking with a friend this
morning about a trial she is going through. It hurts so much right
now. It seems clear what God would have her do, but it also seems
murky emotionally. We both talked of how it will look years from
now, and how God can use these times in our lives to be an
encouragement to others going through similar things. We don't
even have to share all the gory details, just the highlights can be
enough to help another fill their own story into the blanks. We
wonder why God would use things that cut us so deeply? And yet,
by going very, very deep, almost like a root-canal type of digging
into our hearts, God can then move into that emptiness and fill it
up with all that is good and right and true. There are usually years
of infection that need to be cleared out, before God's love can truly
be absorbed into our souls.

*You may never know, but I do, and God does. I hope if I do not
thank you all personally, you will still feel the joy in your heart
you have given to me.*

I have not been able to thank everyone personally for all the help I
have been given. But, I have been able to pass some of that same
help onto others through the years. And hopefully, I will continue

to do that to honor not only Phil's life, but also to honor all those who helped us along the way. If you are one of those, and you are reading this book, "Thank you, from the bottom of my once shattered heart. Thank you for sticking by me and my family through the years. Thank you for your prayers. And may God bless you and yours through the years."

Gift #15 – Seeing the Body of Christ working together as it should.

What tool in God's toolbox has been a handy help on your own journey?

Is there something that you can think of that might be a sweet offering to someone who is hurting right now?

Record today's date and other notes you'd like to make:

The Great

I AM

Two are better than one, because they have a good return for their work: If one falls down, his friend can help him up. But pity the man who falls and has no one to help him up! Also, if two lie down together, they will keep warm. But how can one keep warm alone? Though one may be overpowered, two can defend themselves. A cord of three strands is not quickly broken.
Ecclesiastes 4:9-12 (NIV)

CHAPTER SIXTEEN

If only for this life we have hope in Christ,
we are to be pitied more than all men.
1 Corinthians 15:19 (NIV)

Me

A Small White Star

Wednesday, 23 Jan 2002

*A small white star hung on our Christmas tree this year. It was given to us by a friend. On the star was the word "Hope"...a simple message with **huge** proportions. Next to that star hung a clear, tear-drop ornament, also given to us by a friend. It represents our broken hearts. Side by side they hung–one representing our sadness, the other our strength.*

We got our Christmas pictures back the other day. They included our family picture by the tree that we take every year. The plan was to have a picture from each year, and after 25 years of Christmases, to gather all the pictures and put them into an album. I'm not sure where I'm going with this writing, but I guess I'm thinking about the word hope because of a song I heard this morning. They were singing, "Hope changes everything." I wonder when the people write these songs if they have any idea how they affect the people who listen to them? Songs inspire me, encourage me, make me cry, and make me remember good times and sad. I wanted to come home today and write that verse on a piece of paper and stick it on my computer here. I probably still will, because it takes the cold, hard facts, and it changes the way I look at them, and the outcome of it all.

When I go to my Bible, I usually expect a revelation from God. Also, when I go to God in prayer, I'm expecting Him to teach me something new and something different. Most of the time, that is exactly what I come away with. Not only that, when I go searching in the Word with a thought in mind, I will find that very thought is usually what I end up reading. This may sound strange to you if you have never done it, or if you are not a believer, but I am sharing what is true for me. Sometimes it just happens, and sometimes I search for a key word. Like today, I had the word hope on my mind and I remembered a verse talking about, "without that hope we are to be pitied above all men." I looked up the word "pitied" in the back of my Bible, and it took me right to this verse:

If only for this life we have hope in Christ, we are to be pitied more than all men. 1 Corinthians 15:19 (NIV)

I read what was before this verse and what came after it, and it talked about the resurrection of the dead. It said how some say that there is no resurrection of the dead, and if that is true then not even Christ is raised. This would make our preaching useless and our faith futile. It would make us false witnesses about God, and that those who are dead would be lost. There would be no Hope, no reason to preach God's Word, no changing anything! But Paul goes on to say, Christ has indeed been raised from the dead, and in Christ all will be made alive. He talks about what kind of body we will have. He says the splendor of the Heavenly body is one kind, and the splendor of the earthly body is another. The sun has

151

one kind of splendor, the moon another. Now we have a natural body. When we are raised we will have a spiritual body.

Heaven is as much a part of my world now as this earth is. It's part of my every day, because my son lives there. He moved to Heaven on November 14, 2001. I'd like to visit him, but I can't. I'd like to check how the weather is there. But I guess I don't need to, because I know it's perfect. I'd like to write to Phil, but the U.S. Postal service can only do so much! I'd like to know what Phil does every day. But for now, that is top secret.

"Hope changes everything" because I don't have to look at death as the world does. I can look at it as God does. And I can talk to God anytime, anywhere, and be close to Phil in that way. "Hope changes everything" because even though I am sad, I can have joy. My faith in that Hope is what changes everything about this world. It turns it all inside out and makes sense of things that make no sense. It changes what I value, and how I spend my time. It changes my relationships, and what I want to do with my future. It takes a broken heart and starts to mend it in a way that some may not believe is possible. It gives me the strength to go on, when I'd rather not. It gives me a reason for living when this world seems futile. When nothing else means anything, God's Hope means everything to me. To live without this Hope—well, I say that going through this grief is the most difficult thing I've ever had to do. But what I am thinking now is that to live without Hope would be the most difficult thing to do. With Christ and His eternal Hope, I can do all things.

Today I went to our normal grocery store for the first time since Phil died. I have avoided it for over two months. I've gone to others, avoided shopping, you name it, but I had not returned to the store that Phil and I shopped in together. I went through that entire store today quoting, "Fear not, for I am with you. Be not dismayed, for I am your God." (Isaiah 41:10 NKJV) And, "I can do all things through Christ who strengthens me." (Philippians 4:13 NKJV) Sometimes it is the little things that I need help in, and sometimes the huge eternal issues. But not only is Christ my Hope,

He is my strength through all things. I laugh. I smile. I cry. And I miss. But I am moving forward through this grief with God's help, and I will come out on the other end of it better than when I went in, because I have eternal Hope.

Thanks for "listening" once again,

Diane

Myself

A small white star hung on our Christmas tree this year. It was given to us by a friend. On the star was the word "Hope." Next to that star hung a clear, tear-drop ornament, also given to us by a friend. It represents our broken hearts.

Twelve years later, we still hang that star of Hope and teardrop on our tree. That Hope has carried us through all these years, and continues to. I am grateful for the healing that has come to our once very broken hearts. (When I write the word *hope,* as in eternal *Hope*, I like to use a capital "H." It sets it apart that way.)

They were singing, "Hope changes everything."

I didn't know it then, but I do now. Hope **has** changed everything. Then, I was just hoping it would. Now, I *know* it does. That is what time and experience give us They give us a perspective that we can't get any other way. Recently, our oldest son, Jimm, was going through a hard time at work. He was trying as best he could to resolve the issues, and he called me to talk it through. When we finished our discussion, I told him I only had a couple of things to say. He was doing everything right, and being very professional about it. But because he is only 35, and I remember when I was 35, he has not yet had the opportunity to learn a lot of patience. That was the only thing working against him at this point. Lo and behold, after some time went by, his issue was resolved in a most miraculous way. It just took time, and he gained experience in the process. It's not easy, or fun most times, but it is what it is.

...because it takes the cold, hard facts, and it changes the way I look at them, and the outcome of it all.

The cold hard facts. They were cold, and they were hard, and they certainly were factual. There was no changing what was. The only thing I could do was change the way I looked at it. That took lots of practice. It took putting my trust in a God who wasn't making a whole lot of sense at the time. Those facts are still facts on this day. Our son is still in Heaven, away from us for a time, but we are seeing the outcome of relying on God to get us through all these years. Our hearts are not hard, and they are not cold toward the things of God. Our hearts are much more willing to be with what is, because of our eternal Hope. We are just passing through; we can wait it out.

When I go to my Bible, I usually expect a revelation from God. Also, when I go to God in prayer, I'm expecting Him to teach me something new and something different.

I just wrote about this subject today, in a way, in my SAND Room writings. (thesandroom.com) Why? Because, I have gone to my Bible many, many days, weeks, months and years now. And the enemy STILL tries to get me not to. Why? Because he knows it works. The enemy knows God's Word is powerful! It changes lives, and it heals hearts. It works! We just have to learn to work with it! SAND is an acronym for **S**earching **A**nd **N**oticing the **D**ivine. God wants us to look for Him in all things—in His Word, and in His World. When we do, we will notice Him all around and in us as believers. It might take a little practice, but we'll start to notice Divine moments every single day. Even as recent as this evening, I saw God's protection driving home from my granddaughter's soccer game. My son, Chris, and I were driving side-by-side, a bit distracted, when a car in front of us almost came to a stop, trying to change lanes. We both slowed easily, as it moved over. I felt, in my spirit, God's protection from an accident. I see God working in those moments, and fulfilling the verse, "But seek ye first the kingdom of God, and his righteousness; and all these things shall be added unto you." (Matt. 6:33 KJV) It's not that bad things will never happen again, but it seems less bad things happen, and more Divine moments surround us when we are focused on the things of God in our day—especially when we start in His Word each morning.

"Hope changes everything" because I don't have to look at death as the world does.

The world is a different world than it was 12 years ago. In fact, it was about 12 years ago that the world, especially things here in the U.S., started to change. 9/11 happened, and our country was attacked in a way it never had been before. But as Christians, we don't have to fear things like 9/11, or even the crazy things that are happening now, the way the world does. Jesus conquered death, He took it back from the enemy, and He gave us eternal life. That is our Hope, and that is what changes everything. When we meet people in the world who don't believe in the same Hope we do, it is good to take some time and talk with them about it if they will engage with us in conversation. Because of the prophecies written about in the Bible, there are many who see what is going on in our world today, and match it up with the end times. This subject came up at work the other day. It was a great opportunity to talk about the Hope we can have in Jesus, and how we need not fear, but we need to be ready to meet Him upon His return.

It takes a broken heart and starts to mend it in a way that some may not believe is possible.

It doesn't seem possible in the beginning to ever feel good again. But slowly, over time, God's Hope is like a salve that nurtures and heals what is cracked and broken. There is no other "medicine" quite like it on the market. Oh, there are numbing drugs, and other substances that might seem to help for a bit, but nothing like what we can get from our Savior. He has written out a prescription for us. It is a long one, but it can be filled daily if we will only study what He has written to us in His Word. We are loved from above. We are cared for from above. Let's not settle for the things of this

world to cure our heartache when the Master Physician knows just
what is needed.

*Today I went to our normal grocery store for the first time since
Phil died. I have avoided it for over two months.*

I didn't remember this—that it took over two months just to go
back to the grocery store where we shopped together. Phil and I
spent a lot of time together. He was out of school a lot, and we
were pretty much joined at the hip. Neither one of us minded. We
enjoyed being together. I believe God gave us 5 ½ compacted
years together because He knew I would probably be living the
next 40 without Phil. But that being said, it made it hard, as it does
for all of us, to do the things we did. I can do them now. I still
think about Phil, of course. Those memories don't fade, but they
become less painful and more enjoyable. That's what time and
God do for a person who clings to the promises believers have.

*I will come out on the other end of it better than when I went in,
because I have eternal Hope.*

Here I am, at the other end, practically! Am I better than when I
went in? I believe I am, because of knowing God more intimately
each day. Life is challenging, even today. My parents are aging
and going through difficulties. Friends are hurting, and the
Government shut down this week for the first time in 17 years. It's
a crazy world! But we can stay sane when we know our Savior.
We can be excited for His return. We should look forward to it,
and be prepared. That is what I know more than ever, after coming
out on the other end, and those are very good things to know.

Gift #16 – Beginning to realize that God's Hope holds so much more for us than this world does.

Are you learning how to hold onto what Jesus died to give us, a little bit more each day?

If not, would you be willing to find someone who can share that Hope with you, and spend time with them?

Record today's date and other notes you'd like to make:

The Great

<u>I AM</u>

Not only so, but we also rejoice in our sufferings, because we know that suffering produces perseverance; perseverance, character, and character, hope.
Romans 5:3-5 (NIV)

CHAPTER SEVENTEEN

"Turn to me and have mercy on me; grant your strength to your servant...for you, O Lord, have helped me and comforted me."
Psalm 86:16 (NIV)

<u>Me</u>

How-deee!

Wednesday, 13 Feb 2002

Yes, I'm back! Been to the Grand Ole Opry, twice. Once, for the old-timers, and once for some new-timer—both enjoyable in different ways. The second night we went, there was a fund-raiser put on by Joe Diffe. It was called One Step. It helps support kids who are a bit behind. I believe he has a mentally handicapped child, and so that is where his passion lies. Good music, and a good night. Wynona was even there, and who should join her but her mother, Naomi. She is a walking miracle from what I know. Having had hepatitis, and quitting her singing career, she is now completely cured. It was fun to see them back on stage as mother and daughter.

It's late for me here tonight, since I am still on Nashville time, but of course I feel like writing. I wonder what though.

*Did I have a good time? Well, yes I did, as a matter of fact. Was it difficult? Well, yes it was, as a matter of fact. Had I not been with my best friend, Deb, who understood that, I'm not sure how I would have done. What's so difficult? Well, it's hard to pin down because it's everything and nothing at the same time. It's every song I hear. It's every blue rose I see. It's every meal I eat. It's every young boy I see. It's every mother caring for her child. It's every conversation I have that would lead to Phil, and yet he has never been to Nashville. How could he be there at every turn? Because, **he just is**. He is with me every second of every day, no matter what. I can't escape that by flying across the country and leaving his memories behind me. It just doesn't seem to work that way. Not, at least, for me. He was so much a part of every day I lived, that everything I do now, has a piece of his memory in it.*

Like going to the Grand Ole Opry Mall. It is HUGE! It has every store imaginable, even Hilo Hatties. That is where we bought our Hawaiian shirts when we took the boys to Hawaii last April. Yes, in Nashville! Anyone need a Hawaiian shirt? I walked around the mall a bit, leaving Deb to do some clothes shopping which is not my favorite thing. Then we met up again, and she asked if I was ready to go? More than ready! By the time I got back to the hotel, my emotional gas tank was on empty. It was in the red zone. I felt shaky, needing to refuel desperately, which is exactly what I did. You'd be surprised what an hour with God and His Word can do for an empty emotional tank. It was never more evident to me than it was on this trip. At home, I have learned to adjust. Or maybe I've learned what to avoid. Or maybe I've just been through a lot of the firsts at home. But on the road, in a new place, it is a constant flow of "firsts" that need to be faced, and it drains all tanks and reserves more quickly than you would imagine. We kidded that we did not drive very far in our rental car, only needing a small amount of gas when we got ready to leave to fill up the tank. But I laugh because "I" refueled so many times while we were there. I asked my friend how can having fun be so hard? I don't think either one of us had the answer to that question. I only know that it was, and I only know that she understood it enough to help me through it. I would dive into the Psalms, and read of David's struggles where he was asking God for mercy, help, and strength; and finding it all right there. He received it, and so did I!

I would read Psalms like 86:1-4 (NLT):

"Bend down, O Lord, and hear my prayer:
answer me, for I need your help.
Protect me, for I am devoted to you.
Save me, for I serve you and trust you.
You are my God.
Be merciful, O Lord,
for I am calling on you constantly.
Give me happiness, O Lord,
for my life depends on you.

Oh, I was a pitiful sight! I was drinking in God's Word so I could keep having fun. Crazy, isn't it? But true! I wanted to have fun. I really did. I wanted to enjoy this vacation like so many in the past. But my heart was stretched way beyond where it has ever gone before. I was out there, walking through this grief of only 13 weeks, not on my own strength, but only on the strength that God provided. Oh, I could have done it on my own, perhaps. Some do, or attempt to. But why? Why not retreat to my room, open God's Word and let Him fill my heart to overflowing. Why not ask Him for that help, and receive it? That is what He promised us. That is what I was seeking. I found it. Was it work? Yes, it was! But work that was well worth it.

As I read down further in Psalm 89:1-2 (NIV)

"I will sing of the Lord's great love forever; with my mouth I will make your faithfulness known through all generations. I will declare that your love stands firm forever, that you established your faithfulness in heaven itself."

And verse 15-17 (NIV):

"Blessed are those who have learned to acclaim you, who walk in the light of your presence, O Lord. They rejoice in your name all day long; they exult in your righteousness. For you are their glory and strength..."

That is what I was searching for. That is what I found. This whole grieving process is difficult beyond description. The missing that I feel for Phil...there are no words really. And even if I tried to explain it, just that alone would be longer than my longest e-mail ever, which would be long! It, the grief, the sadness, is with me everywhere, all the time, and even more evident if I think for a moment that I can escape it by leaving home for a bit. It just doesn't work. The only thing that works is to work at it, to pray about it, and ask for all the help I can get from God who provides everything we need. To take that time, to stop, drop, and roll as I have described in earlier e-mails, and let God help me back up on my feet again; however many times in the day it is needed. Wherever I am.

Phil was never in Nashville. He was never at the Grand Ole Opry. He was never even in the state of Tennessee. But he has been there now, because he traveled there in my heart. I took him there. I left memories of him there. And when I return there some day, I will find him there. I will find him there in the memories of the wounded heart that I took there with me this time. I will find him in the progress that I will have made when I travel there again, hopefully not needing to refuel every few hours to just keep walking. I will be glad for that progress, I know that. I will remember when my grief was just in its baby stages, and when it was so hard. I will remember that first vacation trip, and having to come home to his empty bedroom still sitting as he left it. I will remember the sign on the front door for me today, put there by younger Jimm, saying, "Welcome Home Mom! We missed you!" And I will remember thanking God for all the blessings in my life. I will remember sitting in church on my first night back. Jim working in the tech booth, both boys there with me, my sister and her husband, friends all around, and being grateful for all those who surround me.

Yes, I had to stop, drop, and roll when I got back to California. I was out of gas, once again. I stopped in at the ole fillin' station, read the Psalms, and asked God to help me face the fact that Phil was not here to welcome me home—that he never will be again; but that he will welcome me Home to Heaven someday. Maybe he will have a sign that says, "Welcome Home Mom! I've missed you!" Maybe. But probably not, because there are no tears or missing in Heaven. Just tears in Nashville, in airports, and all over this world. But this world is not our home; we are only passing through!

"For physical training is of some value, but godliness has value for all things, holding promise for both the present life and the life to come." 1 Timothy 4:8 (NIV)

I'm in training for the life to come. The life I live here sure is painful at times. But it will be worth it when the door to eternity swings wide open, and Phil is waiting there to greet me. It will all be worth it, as this trip was. It's all part of the preparation, all part of the enjoyment, and all part of the pain.

Good-night for now. I'm tired.

Love, Diane

Myself

Yes, I'm back! Been to the Grand Ole Opry...

It took over two months just to go to the grocery store, and then I attempted Nashville? That seems like a crazy thing to do. But with traveling, it was sort of like needing to get back on the horse. I had done a lot of it with Phil, and without Phil. To quit doing it would be quitting a big part of my life.

*What's so difficult? Well, it's hard to pin down because it's
everything and nothing at the same time.*

How can we understand the workings of a broken heart? Only God
can fully, I suspect. I do understand it a bit better now though.
What I really understand a whole lot better is that the pain doesn't
last forever, but the memories do. Just recently I saw pictures
online of my brother, Howard, and his family at the same exact
place Deb and I visited in Nashville. It didn't throw me for a loop.
I didn't start crying, although that would have been okay, too.
What I did was remember my time there, with my best friend, and
how God got me through those days. That is faith building!

*He is with me every second of every day, no matter what, and I
can't escape that by flying across the country and leaving his
memories behind me.*

Many people say, "Keep busy." We are encouraged to go on trips,
or go shopping, or work a lot. I didn't purposely do these things to
bury the pain, but I did do them along the way, and I found out that
they don't ease the pain one bit. The pain travels with us, stays
with us, and continues on with us if we don't put it to rest. And the
only way to put it to rest is to leave it with God, to take it right into
the Throne Room and lay it at His feet. That is what I did on this
trip, and do to this day. It is the greatest pain relief ever! Yes, it
comes back as any pain does after a fresh "injury." But less and
less through the years.

*By the time I got back to the hotel my emotional gas tank was on
empty.*

It was a horrible feeling. I felt I had to escape the mall, the people,
and the memories. The only way I could do that, in a healthy way,
was to get alone with God. Not even my best friend could comfort
me in those moments. The air in my lungs seemed depleted, it
seemed I was gasping for breath. Deb would leave me alone in our
hotel room, which was very good for me. When she returned, I'm
sure she was relieved that I could breathe again. And we would go

back out into the world, tour around, eat, and then repeat. It was challenging, and strength building, and I wouldn't exchange it for the world now. But at the time, it seemed a little crazy!

At home, I have learned to adjust. Or maybe I've learned what to avoid. Or maybe I've just been through a lot of the firsts at home.

At home, we can keep our world small—same road to the store, same road to church, same road to visit family, etc... It's easy to get stuck on those same roads. Being out of that comfort zone, sort of feels like being thrown into a shark tank. Everything comes too close, seems too scary, and bites too hard. But, it won't always. Maybe it's, eventually, like being in a shark tank, but being inside one of those steal cages. You know the enemy is out there, lurking, but God's protection becomes more and more evident around us, and we know we won't be eaten up by our grief.

I asked my friend how can having fun be so hard?

It helps to have patient family and friends, because we really are not thinking straight. Everything is thrown together and muddled and horrible. It is all SO overwhelming! I can barely explain it in words here. We want to go, and do, and be like before, but it takes more effort than we think we can give. Eventually, we can go, just not do too much. Then we can do, but not be like we were before. And then one day we realize that it's not taking quite the effort it once did to go and do. Eventually, we are able to start to give back what has been given to us—God's healing touch of Hope when all hope seemed lost.

But my heart was stretched way beyond where it has ever gone before.

There were new places, with reminders of everything old. One day, Deb and I were walking through a building in Nashville and she noticed some blue roses in the window of a florist shop. She commented on them, and then she remembered that we had purchased blue roses to throw onto the top of Phil's coffin the day we buried him. OUCH! She wished she had never said anything. I wish she had never said anything then. But today, I remember that moment like it was yesterday and it's not a bad thing; it's a good one. It is now an old reminder of everything that has been made new.

I will remember when my grief was just in its baby stages, and when it was so hard.

I wrote this then, and I'm living it now. Praise God! And Hallelujah! Which is just praising God again!! Why not? He alone has healed my broken Nashville heart. Not with time alone, but with experiencing life again with Him helping me through every step of the way. How can a Mom not be grateful for that? Oh, because He took my son? Of course, that comes to mind. It seems so mixed up. But if we put our trust in God before we know we really can, He will show us in the end that trusting Him is the only thing we *can do* that really works. It's a strange double edged sword. Maybe that's why the Word of God is spoken about as a double-edged sword. It cuts deep, but also heals deep.

I will remember that first vacation trip, and having to come home to his empty bedroom still sitting as he left it.

I don't think I thought about this before I left for vacation—that coming home would also hold unexpected hard things. That is why it is good to not worry about tomorrow, because today holds enough trouble of its own. Each step has to be met when it comes up before us. God gives us the grace we need along the way. He really does know what we need, when we need it, and how to apply it to our lives. Sometimes it doesn't seem/feel like enough, but it is. Wherever God has us, it is for a reason. Our granddaughter, Denell, now sleeps in that very same bedroom that Phil left empty. (Our son and his wife own that house now.) It is filled with girly things, and I'm reminded when I see it how life truly does go on. I know Phil would be pleased that his niece fills our heart with such joy!

I will remember sitting in church on my first night back . Jim working in the tech booth, both boys there with me, my sister and her husband, friends all around, and being grateful for all those who surround me.

It was good to be home. Good to be back in my little comfort zone. But I know now that I had grown immensely by stepping out and taking that trip. Not to escape the pain, but to embrace the pain, and then to continue to embrace the life I had left to live with those I still have left to live it with. We can get blinded to all those blessings, but they are always there. We have to keep looking. I love looking at our boys now, men really, and the lives they are living. Both are devoted husbands and good dads. They have steady jobs that pay the bills, which is a lot to be thankful for. I love their wives. Jimm's wife, Cami, has a heart of gold. She has been a huge support to Jimm. I wish they didn't live so far away in Oregon. Chris' wife, Holly, is a joy. She and Chris work so well together! And even while running a daycare business in their home, she still welcomes my stop-in visits with a smile. Last but not least, I look at our grandchildren! What an amazing blessing they are! The only problem is, they grow too fast. But any of you that are grandparents understand about that. It's not a perfect life, but it is good. Thank You, Jesus, for helping me hang on until the pain eased, and the blessings flowed. You were always there, and I want to always be where You are.

Maybe he will have a sign that says, "Welcome Home Mom! I've missed you!"

That brings a smile to my face even on this day as I read that. And I think about Phil's birthday coming up next week. I see the leaves falling outside, and the pumpkins have started to appear in the stores. It's October once again—and yet, it's not ALWAYS on my mind now. I don't FEAR the 16th coming. I don't WONDER if I will live through it. I KNOW I will! I KNOW God is with me! I KNOW He will continue to carry me until I see Phil again. It is a good KNOWING that we will see each other in Heaven.

Gift #17 – Knowing that we can get through all things, old and new, with the strength of the Holy Spirit, who lives in us.

Where are you most comfortable in your time of grief?

Where would you go that would be a huge stretch for you at this point on your journey?

Record today's date and other notes you'd like to make:

The Great

<u>I AM</u>

"For physical training is of some value,
but godliness has value for all things,
holding promise for both the present life
and the life to come."
1 Timothy 4:8 (NIV)

CHAPTER EIGHTEEN

We love because He first loved us.
1 John 4:19 (NIV)

<u>Me</u>

Prayer

02/15/2002

Unanswered prayer... Is there such a thing? I wonder. It seems so. But it may not be so.

God hears. God responds. So maybe it's just our reaction to His response that leaves us questioning whether we've been heard or not.

The most powerful answer to prayer that I have experienced is asking God to take Phil Home to Heaven. Is there any more difficult prayer than that? Not in my lifetime, I'm sure. Phil asked me if it was okay to ask God for such a thing. He was tired. He was sick. He wanted to be released from his years of suffering. He was ready. We prayed together, asking God to release him from this world. Had I known the finality of that request, I don't think I could have ever asked for it.

You may think it strange that I did not realize that finality. But I didn't. Not until now, and even now I have trouble absorbing that I will never see him again on this earth. At times, it still does not seem real. Then there are times when it does, and I want to scream, cry, and fight against it. There is no fighting against it though. It is. That is final. I will have to learn to live with it–like it or not.

Did God answer our prayer? Yes, He did. Did I pray the wrong prayer? I wonder now. I wanted what was best for Phil. I wanted his suffering to end. But I didn't want this. I wanted to have Phil here with me, for as long as I lived. That is what we expect from our children–that they will leave this earth long after our departure. It is not always so. There is no right order to things, only God's order.

I prayed for Phil's healing too. I prayed for many years, more times than I could ever count. I prayed, and I prayed, and I prayed. Where was God then? Did He hear this mother's cries for help? I believe He did. He never left us. He continued to show us the way through. Was His answer, "No" on this one? Well, it was in a way, and it wasn't in a way.

Right before Phil died, he told me that God was healing him, that he felt better, that tomorrow he would feel good. Twenty minutes later he was gone. HEALED, and taken Home. Did I pray the wrong prayer all those years? I asked for healing. I got it. But I never prayed for healing and a long life. I never prayed that. Was that a mistake? Are there mistakes? Are our prayers that effective that they can actually change what may or may not happen? The Bible says they are. Ezekiel prayed for more time and was given 15 more years. If I had asked for healing and a long life, would Phil still be with us? I will only know the answer to that question when I see him again. And then, it really won't matter one bit.

Do I struggle with this? Recently, I have. It's just part of the thought process that I go through these days. Thoughts can be a powerful thing, for the good, and for the bad. When I am tired, my thoughts go places that are very destructive.

Rest is very important. Not getting overly tired saves a lot of heartache for me. Keeping my boundaries in place helps me keep my sanity when I want to fight against what is. What's done is done now. There is no going back. There are no more lessons that I will be able to teach Phil, no more talks about life here and life in Heaven with my son, no more doctor's appointments, and blood transfusions, pain and sickness. There will be no more trips to the movies, or cheeseburgers before Wednesday night church–none of that.

I can't change a thing, except what will happen now. What will I do with what I've been given and with what I've been taught? How will I use it? Will it be wasted, or will it be used? If I didn't realize the power of prayer to its full extent while Phil was still with me. I realize it now, because in some ways it is all I have now. That is not to disregard those that surround me with their love and support. That is not to disregard the beauty of this world, and the enjoyment of this world. I'm not disregarding anything that God has blessed me with. But without prayer, without being able to be in God's presence and absorb His love, the rest would not even exist for me.

In 1 John 4:19 (NIV) it says, "We love because He first loved us." When we realize the love of God, when we feel the depth of all that He offers us, and the faithfulness and gentleness of His Spirit, it brings everything else in our life into a clearer realization. It makes it possible to enjoy all that we have, even in the deepest grief. It makes it possible to see the Hope in what seems like a hopeless situation. It lifts us out of the pit of desperation for what has been lost, and shows us all that we have gained.

God's love is the root of all that is good in this world. Without it, we would topple. Even those that don't know God's love, really do.

They may not be aware of where it comes from, or want to admit that there is something there that they cannot understand. But it doesn't diminish the fact that it is there—that God's love flows through this world, unseen and yet very seen if we are looking for it.

I rest in that love. I let it surround me when the hole in my heart is so enormous nothing could ever fill it. I stop fighting what is, and relax in what will be because God is in control. He always has been. He always will be.

When our prayers seem unanswered, they are not. They are simply answered in a way that we cannot, nor will we ever, understand on this earth. Should I have prayed for a long life for Phil, not just his healing? Would that have changed a thing? I don't know. But it really doesn't matter. God knows best, and I trust Him for that. He is all-knowing. He knows every hair on my head, and He knows what I am going to pray before I even pray it. He knows the answers before we even ask.

How can we understand that? We can't. We never will. But we can trust it. God is good, even when things are bad. God is sure, and true, and right. Always! Nothing else on this earth, no one else on this earth, can claim that. If we are holding onto anything else, it will eventually fail us. It can't help it. It is flawed, because sin entered our lives and things have never been the same again. Answered prayer or unanswered prayer—it's all the same. It is simply a conversation that we have with God about all the happenings in our life, (like we have with our very best friend) and trusting the outcome to the only One who has all the answers.

We can't beat ourselves up about any of it. We can only work to establish a relationship with our Creator. Drawing close to Him as He draws close to us, and finding our peace and contentment there. It can always be found there. We just need to seek it.

I don't want to beat myself up because my prayers may have been off, or incorrect from my point of view. My point of view means little; it's only important to me. God's point of view and His decisions are always correct. I can lean back into that thought and relax.

Myself

Unanswered prayer... Is there such a thing?

I used to wonder. Now I realize God has three answers to prayer. *Yes. No. Wait.* It's really that simple. God hears everything. ALL our prayers. He hears them before we voice them. It's just that we have to learn to live in His answers—one of the three. *Yes* is usually the easy answer. *No* can be hard, but at least we got an answer. *Wait* seems to be the most difficult because we feel unheard.

The most powerful answer to prayer that I have experienced is asking God to take Phil Home to Heaven. Is there any more difficult prayer than that?

To this day, I can't believe I actually asked God to take Phil Home. It was at Phil's request. I never would have asked that for myself— to relieve me of the duty of caring for him. But I did ask it for my son. Just writing that now, I wonder how selfish that was of me. I didn't consult with Phil's dad. I have to believe he would have gone along with Phil's wishes also. We have talked about it many times since. We love Phil so much, and he had battled so long and so hard. Why would we not want relief for him? But I know it was the Holy Spirit praying through me in that moment. Otherwise, no mother could ever pray that prayer. And it was also that I didn't realize what I was really asking. I had never lived without a child on this earth before. Which makes me wonder... Would I be able to be unselfish enough if I needed to pray that prayer again? I would hope so.

You may think it strange that I did not realize that finality.

Sitting on the edge of my bed in the morning, about 12 hours before Phil left us, I prayed to God. I told Him I didn't know how much longer this would go on, but for Him to please give me the strength I needed to do what needed to be done. I had no idea what was coming that very day, or what that even meant. God's protective fog really does help sometimes. He helps us keep putting one foot in front of the other when we lean on Him. I was leaning HARD!

At times it still does not seem real and then there are times when it does.

The reality is here. There is no question in my mind 12 years later about what has happened, and what that looks like, feels like, and requires. When it fully set it, I'm not sure. I think because it's gradual. There is no one day. It comes in like ocean waves and knocks us off our feet. Then the wave goes out again, allowing us to stand up. We feel our whole world shifting under our feet. It feels strange, and we wonder about how it all works. Then another huge wave lands on us, and we fall to our knees, wondering if this one will surely do us in. But it doesn't. And now, all these years later, the waves are calmer. We don't have to fear each moment thinking it will kill us. We can know that we have lived many days, months, and years, and God has seen us through. And we can be grateful. Just today, I visited Phil's gravesite. I rarely go there. Not out of disrespect, but just because I'd rather look up when remembering him, rather than down. Standing there with my friend, Lynn, today, I talked of that terribly difficult day when we watched his casket being lowered into the ground. I told her how I hoped without knowing then. But now I *know* and *live in* that Hope. The years, and God, have taught me that. I described our trip to the cemetery today in a way I never had before. I told her we were going to where Phil's pre-resurrected body was. I've never heard it put that way before. But that is truly what I believe on this day. As we drove out of the graveyard, I said, "I'll see you soon, Phil." With all the things happening in our world today, I believe Jesus' return isn't far away!

I wanted to have Phil here with me, for as long as I lived. That is what we expect from our children—that they will leave this earth long after our departure.

In the day and age we live in, parents usually die before their children. It wasn't that long ago that that wasn't true. People had very large families, and many children preceded their parents on the trip Home to Heaven. As we wound our way out of the cemetery today, we saw four small grave markers. We stopped, knowing they were probably small children in one family. All four of the children had died at less than three months of age, over a span of 13 years in the late 1800's. We got out of the car to see if there had been any child buried there that had lived into adulthood. There were two others buried there, along with the parents of all the children. One of the adult children had died two years before the mother. The other one had died the same year as her, but we didn't know the month so we didn't know who had gone first. As moms ourselves, we felt for her and all her earthly heartache. Just writing that, I wonder if it is another one of Satan's lies to make us turn our back on God because death is seemingly so unfair. It just doesn't seem right—that's because we were not created to die. But since Adam and Eve were disobedient and ate fruit from the tree of knowledge of good and evil, death is here. (Genesis 3:6) We now have to turn to Jesus to bring us safely Home to Heaven. He is our only choice. Our best choice. All will be well one day!

I prayed for Phil's healing too. I prayed for many years, more times than I could ever count. I prayed, and I prayed, and I prayed. Where was God then?

God heard those desperate prayers. That we can know. It probably broke His heart to know the tremendous amount of pain that was coming, as it did when His own Son gave up His life for us on the Cross. But Jesus did it because of the joy set before Him. He would be saving us for all of eternity, and returning to His Father in Heaven soon. Phil had a lot of joy waiting for him in Heaven, too, as do all our loved ones who love Jesus! We can be happy for them, even in the missing.

Are our prayers that effective that they can actually change what may or may not happen?

I have to believe prayers are super effective! Phil suffered for 5 ½ years. Three hours after we asked God for his suffering to be over, it was. Strange answer to a strange prayer, I know. But effective? Yes!

No more trips to the movies, or cheeseburgers before Wednesday night church–none of that.

I included this here because it reminded me of a conversation I had with Phil one Wednesday night on our way to church. We had stopped for cheeseburgers, and Phil wanted to know if there was anything more he needed to do to get into Heaven. Can you imagine having a conversation like that with one of your children over a cheeseburger? Serious stuff. For sure! But it wasn't a time of tears, and woefulness. It was a time of sharing the Hope and confidence that we can have in our Savior. My heart breaks for the child who cannot turn to their parents and ask about their eternity without receiving a Hope-filled answer. Recently I heard of a conversation between a young four year old and her mom. She asked, "Mom, who made people?" The mom didn't have an answer for her. Her mother had once believed, but was now refusing to embrace the Truth she had been taught. Where does that leave that precious child in her own thoughts? We need to pass on godly wisdom to the next generation. It is our responsibility to give them the Hope they need in this fallen world. I know this little girl's grandmother prays for the whole family, daily.

What will I do with what I've been given, and with what I've been taught? How will I use it? Will it be wasted, or will it be used?

Well, for one, here I am on this day, writing. So much water has gone under the bridge since I asked these questions. Talks in front of groups, talks one on one, stories written, songs written and recorded, prayers said, and bedside vigils. Does any of it make it worth the death of our son? Most would say NOT! And of course if I could have chosen another way, I would have. But we have to do the best with what God has given us. That is all my heart desires each day~to be in God's will, until I am in His arms.

But without prayer, without being able to be in God's presence and absorb His love, the rest would not even exist for me.

What does this mean? It means that going boldly into the Throne Room of God in prayer is where it all happens for me. That's where peace is found. That's where Hope is found! I love these words: "Those who live in the shelter of the Most High will find rest in the shadow of the Almighty. This I declare of the Lord: He alone is my refuge, my place of safety; he is my God, and I am trusting him." Psalm 91:1-2 (NLT)

This very morning I woke up, and I went right into that Throne Room almost before my eyes were open. I want to practice that more, and more, and more each day. I want my first waking thought to be Heavenly focused and not on this world. I am learning it is the best place to be in our heart, when this world gets crazier and crazier.

Thank you, Phil, for making my heart miss you *so* much, that my *only* choice is Jesus! It is the best gift any child could ever give a parent! And thank You, Jesus, for the Cross. I am so grateful that right outside my bedroom window there is a telephone pole. I see it as a gift from God. When I wake each morning, I see that "Cross" first thing, and I can use it as a reminder of where my focus should be each day. Because of the blood of our Lord, shed on the Cross, we have Hope for each day. There is nothing else like it!

Gift #18 – The all consuming saving knowledge of our Hope in Jesus!

What has happened with your prayer life on this journey? Do you pray more or less?

If you could ask one prayer of God today, what would it be?

Record today's date and other notes you'd like to make:

The Great

I AM

Pray in the Spirit at all times and on every occasion. Stay alert and be persistent in your prayers for all believers everywhere.
Ephesians 6:18 (NLT)

CHAPTER NINETEEN

He does not ignore those who cry to him for help.
Psalm 9:12b (NLT)

Me

Have You Ever?

Saturday, 23 Feb 2002

Have you ever heard of the book of Zephaniah? It's close to the end of the Old Testament. I can't say I remember much, but it's vaguely familiar. Maybe my memory is not what it used to be. I am over 40!

Anyway, it's there in the Bible. It only has three chapters, and it's probably not the most exciting read. In fact, it paints a pretty dark picture of the end times. Is this what you want to start your day with?! How did I happen upon it this morning? Do you really want to hear this sad tale? If so, read on.

As my heart catches up with my head, it has become heavier. The last few days I have not felt well. I've been tired—just more than normal. But this morning, I woke with a lighter feeling inside. It was quite noticeable, and I was pleased, to say the least. I even woke earlier than I normally do on a Saturday, so I decided to get up and get some coffee, and then return to bed for some quiet time with my cup of coffee.

Down the hall I went. But I stopped, and I turned into Phil's room. Why would I want to do that when I was just feeling better? I went in. I longed to smell him, and to draw him in. So I put my face down to his comforter and breathed in his scent. My heart ached and the tears began to fall. I turned to his dresser and picked up his watch—the one he so happily bought in Hawaii in April. I could not let it go. I gripped it, as the tears just poured out, unstoppable. It took a while before I could put the watch back down and make my way into the kitchen for my coffee. Continuing to cry, I got my cup, heated the water, put in the International powder I like, opened the door for Phil's dog to be able to go out, and made my way back to my bedroom, an emotional mess! What had I done to myself? Why had I opened this floodgate when the morning had started out so well? Why would anyone do that? I really don't know.

Upon returning to bed, I set my coffee down and grabbed my Bible. Not that I could read it, because I couldn't see through the tears. I opened it, but couldn't focus. Once again, I cried out to God at this point, calling for His help, knowing I needed rescuing. Yes, I was drowning in my tears, and I needed a life preserver to be tossed to me. I couldn't pray. I could only call for help! It did not take long for that help to arrive. My eyes started to focus on a small Cross that we have hung on the wall at the foot of our bed. It's one Jim has had since before we ever met. It's just a simple brass Cross about 10 inches tall. When my eyes fell on that Cross, this peace filled me almost instantly and the tears stopped. I could not take my eyes off of it for quite a long time. I didn't want to, because it had transformed my agony so quickly. I didn't want to let it go from my sight.

I then stopped calling for help, because I no longer needed it, but started thanking God for helping me. Once again, He pulled me from the dark pit, and placed me back on higher ground. You may say, how can that be so? How can looking at that Cross change everything so quickly? I don't have all the answers. I only know what is, and that is what I share with you. Mainly, because God was once again teaching me that when we call upon Him, He will be found by us.

Finally, I reached for my cup of coffee, figuring I could drink it while I gazed upon the Cross. So I did that. When my coffee was finished, I was ready to look away from the Cross. I looked where I had opened my Bible up to in my flood of tears. It was Zephaniah. I started reading, asking God to speak to me through His Word, even though it didn't seem like the most appropriate place to be reading. Normally, I turn to the Psalms. But I just kept reading, and then I read chapter three. Let me share with you what I found there:

Verse 3:17 (NIV)
"The Lord your God is with you,
 he is mighty to save.
 He will take great delight in you,
 he will quiet you with his love,
 he will rejoice over you with singing."

In the book of Zephaniah! After all the doom and gloom painted in chapters one and two, God rescues! Just as He had rescued me! He had thrown down His life preserver in the form of a Cross, because I was drowning in my puddle of tears, and He had saved me! As I read, "he will quiet you with his love," that is exactly what He had done. He quieted my sobbing with the love that was shown on the Cross. Even though I didn't understand all that as it was happening this morning, that is what He did, explaining it to me later in Zephaniah.

Is God singing? I don't know. I can't say as I heard Him, but my heart is singing now! Do you know how comforting it is to know

*that when my heart is breaking, and I think I can't stand another
minute of this pain, God will provide a way of escape just by
calling out to Him? Does this still amaze me? Yes, it does, and I
am more in awe of God each and every time it happens. I get to
that point of suffering, and in that agony I think that, this time, I
am going down, never to emerge again, and I am rescued! Yes,
RESCUED!! I want you to know that!*

Down further in Zephaniah 3 it says:

*Verse 18 (NIV)
"The sorrows for the appointed feasts
     I will remove from you;
     they are a burden and a reproach to you."*

*To me that means that all my sorrow, and all the things that I feel I
am missing in the coming years—Phil's graduation from high
school, or even college, his wedding day, the children he may have
had, the uncle he would have been to Jimm and Chris' children,
the life he would have enjoyed. God will take care of all of that.
The things that I thought were going to happen in Phil's life, and
the sorrow that that brings me to be missing it, will be removed by
God. It won't matter in the end.*

*Verse 20 (NIV)
At that time I will gather you;
     at that time I will bring you home.
I will give you honor and praise
     among all the people of the earth
when I restore your fortunes
     before your very eyes.*

*God will bring me Home. And all that has been taken from me on
this earth, my fortunes (which are not money and possessions but
those that I love) will be restored to me right before my very eyes.
A friend recently wrote to me and said she would like to be there to
witness my reunion with Phil. I enjoyed that thought, that she just
may be there to witness that. I know she will be among those*

resurrected, but she may be so busy greeting those she knows who have gone on ahead of her, she won't have time for my reunions.

I just glanced at the clock and it is only 9:12. It reminds me of that Army commercial that says they do more before 9:00 a.m. than most people do all day! I laugh. Normally, I don't do much before noon. But this morning, God met me once again, and taught me before the day even began that He is mighty to save. God showed me I can walk through the rest of this day transformed by His love, filled with His peace, and able to face this sorrow one more day. Phil would be glad to know that the God He lives with in Heaven is taking care of his mom on this earth until we are reunited. I think he must know that. But I won't know until I get there myself.

Have a wonderful Saturday. Thanks for sharing my morning with me.

Love, Diane

Myself

As my heart catches up with my head, it has become heavier.

Grieving takes such a long, long, long time. When we think we are almost to the bottom of the darkness, there is still more. I don't tell you this to discourage you, but to prepare you if you are on your way. Don't feel alone. Don't think that you are the only one who isn't strong enough to withstand the ferociousness of this storm that is beating against you, and knocking you down over and over again. I hate to say it, but it is normal. But this storm, too, shall pass. Please hang in there. That's why I am writing this book, to prepare you, so with God, you will not fear. He will bring you through. My mom was always one to tell me to prepare ahead for moments that might throw me off balance. She said if you set your boundaries ahead of time, think it out, you won't lose your head in the heat of the moment. You might be able to guess, she was talking to me in my dating years. But it worked! It also worked this last Thanksgiving with not over-eating. I played the scene out ahead of time about how much I wanted to eat. When I got to work the next day and everyone was bemoaning how much they had eaten, I didn't have to. God had helped me in that moment of overeating temptation.

I longed to smell him, and to draw him in. So I put my face down to his comforter and breathed in his scent.

These are wonderful, terrible, very disturbing moments—but everyone who grieves will have them. To still have that lingering scent of our loved ones is a precious gift. I'm so glad God gave us smell; it is so powerful. It is also very painful. But it is part of the process of letting go. Some hold onto their loved-ones clothing for a long time, needing that comfort of smell. That's okay. As long as we are listening and being obedient to God when it is time to move on.

What had I done to myself? Why had I opened this floodgate when the morning had started out so well? Why would anyone do that? I really don't know.

Was it a smart thing to do? Probably not; it's best to stay on a good path if we are on one. But God did have a powerful lesson in it for me through Zephaniah. Did He have that planned out and lead me into Phil's room that morning, or did He plan the rescue when He knew I couldn't resist the temptation to go into his room and breathe Him in? What came first—the chicken or the egg? Well, the chicken of course, that God created. God already knew I was going to make that choice, and He meets us every step along the way. We can trust Him for that, even if our choices are not in our best interest. He will find us and pull us out of the pit when we call to Him for help.

Upon returning to bed, I set my coffee down and grabbed my Bible. Not that I could read it, because I couldn't see through the tears.

When I read this, I marvel that I even had a sense about me to grab for my Bible. Maybe it was already becoming such a morning habit, that I knew eventually I would be reading it, even if I couldn't in that moment. Healthy spiritual habits can go a long way. We need to start forming them. They will carry us through many a hard time.

I couldn't pray. I could only call for help! It did not take long for that help to arrive.

This line surprised me today. I realize now that I WAS PRAYING. It's good to know that prayers don't have to be formal, long, or complicated, etc... They can simply be a call for help to the One who always hears us.

When my eyes fell on that Cross, this peace filled me almost instantly and the tears stopped.

Miraculous! That's what this was! There wouldn't have been anything else on this earth, no drug, no drink, no word of encouragement from a friend, nothing, that could have taken away the pain I felt in my heart in those moments. And yet, the Cross did. A peace, that surpasses understanding filled me, and I knew it was Heaven sent. I love a God who can reach down from Heaven and fill us with such peace by simply willing it to be so. God was also showing me, to watch where we put our **focus.** When I focused on the grief, I found agony. When I focused on the Cross, I found relief. The circumstances remained the same. My heart condition changed!

I then stopped calling for help, because I no longer needed it, but started thanking God for helping me.

When God turns our sorrow into peace, only gratefulness should follow that! I'm glad I was giving thanks. Sometimes I forget to thank God for things. I'm still working on that. It is so important each and every day. It makes me chuckle a bit just now, because I think about that Cross again, the one I see upon waking each morning in our new home. It may be a stretch, but these little things can help us remember to give thanks to Jesus for all He died to give us. The busy world we live in can crowd out all the ways God will show Himself to us each day.

Do you know how comforting it is to know that when my heart is breaking, and I think I can't stand another minute of this pain, God will provide a way of escape just by calling out to Him?

I have needed this so many times over the past 12 years! I needed a way of escape, as we all do who grieve, and go through so many other painful things in life. We need a way out. Too many times we look for the way out in unhealthy choices. They seem easier for some reason. Maybe because of the old adage, if it seems too good to be true, it probably is. Satan lies to us and makes promises to us that are untrue. He wants us to choose his quick and easy way in a bottle, or pills, or sex, or food. Something damaging. It can bring some instant relief. But in writing that, I think about the day I looked at the Cross on our wall in my agony. There could have been no more instant relief than the Cross brought on that day. So Satan lies again, God is faster, greater, better, and more complete than anything the enemy has to offer us!! We just have to **choose Jesus first**!! He will come through for us!

The things that I thought were going to happen in Phil's life, and the sorrow that that brings me to be missing it, will be removed by God. It won't matter in the end.

Honestly, it's begun to not matter. That sounds harsh to even write that. I don't know all that God is doing, of course, but I see more and more of the big picture. Whatever it seems Phil is missing here on earth by leaving so soon, seems insignificant to what he is experiencing now in Heaven. And whatever we think we are missing, like Phil's graduation, or wedding, or children...may never have been meant to be. His life plan was perfectly in God's Hands. If it was cut short, then who had the power to do that? No one did, not even Satan. So it wasn't cut short, it was exactly what it was supposed to be. There never would have been a wedding, or children. Because if these events were supposed to be, they would have been. Period. God wins. Satan loses! All, who will believe get to go Home one day and rejoice in God's promises of an eternal life together. Amen!

God will bring me Home. And all that has been taken from me on this earth, my fortunes (which are not money and possessions but those that I love) will be restored to me right before my very eyes.

"Right before my very eyes." I have to keep my eyes wide open for all that God is restoring, so as not to miss it. I am getting better at that each day. I am seeing more and more of God's blessings. I am practicing watching for Him, and He is making Himself more and more clear. I LOVE that. The Holy Spirit helps in this department too. He is inside all of us who believe Jesus Christ is our Savior. He gently prods us with, "Look there, did you see Me at work?" Or, "Listen, do you hear Me?" Or, "Breathe Me in, I am with you always." We have not been left alone. Jesus promised us that before He left, and He can be trusted to keep all of His promises. If God can't be trusted, then He's not God, and none of this matters anyway. There is no gray area here!

God showed me I can walk through the rest of this day transformed by His love, filled with His peace, and able to face this sorrow one more day.

One more day. One day at a time. That's it right there, the grief walk. No jumping ahead three days, or three weeks, or three years. It just doesn't work that way. But day by day, God will grow us and teach us and help us. That is how it is supposed to work. If God instantly took the pain away, then He might instantly take the love away. Wouldn't He have to, for it to work? And if He takes the love that we feel away for the person we are missing, then the richness of this life goes with it. We have to love deeply for life to mean anything at all. God knows what He is doing, even when it hurts beyond measure.

Gift #19 – Finding God's pain relief is better than anything this world can provide.

Have you found yourself in that moment when it seems life can't go on, but it does?

When you came out on the other side, how has it built your faith in what God can do?

Record today's date and other notes you'd like to make:

The Great

<u>I AM</u>

"The Lord your God is with you,
the Mighty Warrior who saves.
He will take great delight in you,
in his love he will no longer rebuke you,
but will rejoice over you with singing."
Zephaniah 3:17 (NIV)

CHAPTER TWENTY

*I know very well how foolish the message of the cross sounds to
those who are on the road to destruction.*
1 Corinthians 1:18 (NLT)

<u>Me</u>

Foolishness

Saturday, 30 Mar 2002

*The Cross is foolishness to those that don't believe in it. It is! It
says so in the Bible.*

*Foolishness. All of it, unless you've taken that step of faith. Then,
and only then, do the Scriptures start to make sense. Why?
Because God speaks to our spirits, and not with human wisdom.*

1 Corinthians 2:13-14 (NLT)
*"When we tell you this, we do not use words of human wisdom. We
speak words given to us by the Spirit, using the Spirit's words to
explain spiritual truths. But people who aren't Christians can't
understand these truths from God's Spirit. It all sounds foolish to*

*them because only those who have the Spirit can understand what
the Spirit means."*

*Sounds like a secret society doesn't it? Believe me, I know. I've
been outside that door, wondering what was going on inside. It
was years ago, but I still remember it well. I was thinking about
how crazy this world really seemed. I mean, we come here, we live
80-90 years and then we die. What's it all for?*

*The reason I am writing
once again is probably
because tomorrow is
Easter. Last Easter, our
family was together—all
five of us. The day before
Easter, which was April
14th, Phil was baptized in
our neighbor's hot tub.
The poster-sized picture
of him, right after his
baptism, hangs here by my desk. It is probably my favorite picture
of him of all times. He is filled with joy! The day after Easter, we
left for Hawaii—Jim and I, and our three boys. Phil was very sick,
and I truly didn't know if he would live through our ten-day
vacation. I was looking at those pictures yesterday and saw the
bruises all over his legs from a lack of platelets. We had a doctor
lined up over there, should we need one. But we never did.
Actually, Phil refused to even think about doctors in Hawaii. I
don't blame him.*

*The pictures show the fun that we had, but they don't tell the whole
story. I often wondered, as we were surrounded by vacationers, if
any of them had any idea why we were there? How could they
know? They didn't know our hearts were heavy because this
vacation had been booked on the promise that should Phil relapse
again, we would take the whole family to Hawaii. Phil wanted to
see Hawaii before he died. It was one of the things on his "list."*

Now, here we are, a year later. Phil has been gone 4½ months, and we are celebrating Easter without him. But not really; he is with us because he will always be in our hearts. But he is also with Jesus, his Savior and ours.

I was just out at Phil's grave for the first time since November. I told you I don't visit graveyards often. At long last his marker has been placed. It seemed to have gotten lost somewhere after we were told it had been delivered. But that's another story. It is there now, and I went out on this beautiful, sunny California day to visit. There it was. I wondered how I would react. I really didn't know. I wondered if I would once again feel that sickness in the pit of my stomach as I pictured Phil in his shorts and t-shirt under that dirt/lawn. I wondered...and I waited. And I stood there, and I looked around at the green hills, the traffic, the other graves, and all I kept thinking was, he's not here. He's just not here. And he doesn't miss being here either. He doesn't miss the hustle and bustle of this world we live in. He doesn't miss the body that is in this grave that caused him such suffering. He doesn't miss anything. He doesn't care that I went and got flowers to put on his grave to spruce it up today, although I enjoyed the experience because I was doing something for him once again. But he doesn't care.

This is not a bad thing, but a good thing. When I stood there before and the picture of Phil in that grave came into my mind, it was almost more than I could stand. But this time was different. This time, God gave me such a peace that I was almost numb. I forced myself to think about his body and his shorts and his t-shirt...still nothing. He wasn't there.

Others around me were visiting their loved ones. I could see the tears, and hear the sniffles. And I wanted so much to say, "They're not here." Is that cold of me? Heartless? I'm not sure, except that I was glad for the peace—for the knowing that the only thing this grave holds is the remains of what was once Phil. His spirit had moved on to a much better place; a place we cannot even imagine.

That "place," Heaven, is what Easter is all about. That is why we had Holy Week. That is why I spent almost every morning this week starting out my day in prayer and meditation thinking about this final week of Christ's life. That is why we attended Good Friday service last night and pounded a nail, signifying our sins, into the wooden Cross that had been placed by the stage. In the darkness, we walked forward and remembered what Jesus Christ has done for us. That is why we celebrate tomorrow, because tomorrow is Resurrection Sunday. After three days, Christ was no longer in His grave. He had conquered death. He had given us the Hope we all longed for—a way around what seemed and was, so final.

That is why I can stand over Phil's grave, place flowers in the holders, and look around me with peace in my heart and say, "Phil is not here." Yes, his body is here, and will be until Christ returns, but his spirit has moved on to a better place. I can rest assured in that. I saw it leave. I was there, I saw what remained. Even his dog knew something had happened. Shortly after Phil died, his dog Dackel jumped on his bed, went to his cheek to lick him, stopped, and turned around, and left before doing so. Phil was no longer there and she knew it. I don't know how dogs know that.

On Phil's grave marker it says, "For to me to live is Christ, and to die is gain." Philippians 1:21 (NIV)

As I left the cemetery and got into my car, I pulled out my Bible and turned to that passage; only I didn't read that. I was led to read a little farther down where it says:

"Dearest friends, you were always so careful to follow my instructions when I was with you. And now that I am away you must be even more careful to put into action God's saving work in your lives, obeying God with deep reverence and fear." Philippians 2:12 (NLT)

Verses 16-18 (NLT)
"Hold tightly to the word of life, so that when Christ returns, I will

be proud that I did not lose the race and that my work was not useless. But even if my life is to be poured out like a drink offering to complete the sacrifice of your faithful service (that is, if I am to die for you), I will rejoice, and I want to share my joy with all of you. And you should be happy about this and rejoice with me."

Phil's life, to me, seems like a drink offering that was poured out. His 16 years here were for a reason, and I have already seen so many of those reasons come to light. So many of them I will never see until my time on earth is through. I can't say that I am "happy about this." But I do rejoice. Phil completed his race. I told him that today, standing there at his grave. I told him that he had done a good job, and that his job was finished. He was faithful. My life will be forever changed because he lived, and I don't want his work to be useless. He would not want that either after everything he went through here on earth. He did not choose to be sick, but he made the most out of what was given to him.

I made some notes in the final week of Phil's life. Quickly jotted down so that I would be able one day to go back and read them. I read that this morning. I also read some poetry that I had written when it looked as if he was not going to make it. I had not re-read that up until today, either. Both helped me, because there were things that I had forgotten. It was comforting because so many of the memories that I had were foggy, and this brought them to light. It showed me that there were things said that needed to be said, but I had forgotten had been said. There were things done that needed to be done, and prayers prayed that needed to be prayed, and they had been. God was with us, and by re-reading these things, it helped me to see that. One of the things that I noticed in my notes was how ready he was to leave this world behind. The only thing keeping him here was us. I read what I had written about how he seemed sad because he was thinking of not seeing everyone much longer. He had told me that he felt selfish because he wanted to go. He told me a couple of times to "tell everyone I said good-bye." I wrote that he was tired and he had said he'd rather go now, because this was too hard. He said, "I just want us all to go together."

*He had the struggle of wanting to go, but wanting to stay—not knowing for sure what Heaven was going to be like, but not wanting to remain here either. He just wanted us to all go together. Don't we all? But that was not to be. We must remain here and continue on with our work; our race. Phil ran his, and he ran it well. There was probably a time when Phil thought the Cross was foolishness too. I don't know exactly when he came to know Christ. But I know that he did. I know that he was happy to be baptized last year. And I know that as we read the Scriptures to him as he lay dying, they meant everything to him. EVERYTHING! He told me that he wished he had read more. Suddenly it all made sense to him. There was not one ounce of **foolishness** in it. It spoke right to his heart and helped him journey Home.*

Now I read the Scriptures with the same hunger that Phil had on his final days here, because they mean everything to me. Jim even said that this week, this Holy Week, has meant more to him than ever before because of all we have gone through with Phil.

This is no game. This is the real thing, and we are feeling it deeply like never before. When we attend church tomorrow and we celebrate our Risen Lord, we will feel a sense of joy and peace and Hope that only God can provide, and we know it. We know it from the bottom of our hearts.

The Bible says:

"Hear, O Israel! The LORD is our God, and LORD alone. And you must love the LORD with all your heart, all your soul, and all your strength." Deuteronomy 6:4-5 (NIV)

*That is made easier when part of your heart already lives in Heaven with our Risen Lord. Believe me. God has our attention, as he had Phil's, so completely, on his last few days on this earth. The Cross is not foolishness to a dying boy, **or** to his parents!*

Have a Joyous Easter!
Love, Diane

Myself

Foolishness. All of it, unless you've taken that step of faith. Then and only then do the Scriptures start to make sense.

The Scriptures not only start to make sense, they come alive. They mean everything. Without them, there is no Hope. With them, there is everything! Grief can do this. Or, grief can do the opposite. It becomes a choice we make along the way, to turn to God, or turn away from Him. But God never turns away from us. He is unchanging, and He is there for us when we are ready.

Sounds like a secret society doesn't it? Believe me, I know. I've been outside that door, wondering what was going on inside.

How amazing it is when we give our hearts to Jesus, and things start to line up the way they should. I talk to so many who are confused about what to believe. It's not really something we can figure out on our own. It can only be understood when we allow God's Holy Spirit inside of us to teach us. It's not a brain thing, it's a spiritual thing. If we try to figure it out before we "enter in," we will be left on the outside wondering about it all.

The poster-sized picture of him, right after his baptism, hangs here by my desk. It is probably my favorite picture of him of all times.

We moved into an RV, and stored the picture for ten years. Now that we are back on solid ground, in a condo, it hangs in our bedroom. It is still amazing to see how healthy Phil looked after being baptized, although he was very sick at the time. His young friend, Kendra, told her mom, upon seeing the picture, "That is the first time I've ever seen the Holy Spirit shining through a person!"

Phil wanted to see Hawaii before he died. It was one of the things on his "list."

We probably all have some sort of "Bucket List." Hawaii was on Phil's, so we went. What a blessed time that was with our family, but oh soooo difficult. The reason we were there made it hard, but God took good care of us each day. Those memories are so important as the years go on. While we sat discussing which coffin to buy for Phil, that vacation came up in my thinking. Many would purchase expensive coffins to honor their loved ones. I remember telling the funeral director, "We took Phil to Hawaii." We didn't spend a lot on his coffin; we spent it on him instead, while he was still with us. That is one thing I have never regretted.

Phil has been gone 4½ months, and we are celebrating Easter without him. But not really; he is with us because he will always be in our hearts.

I may have mentioned this before, but when I say, "He is with us," I don't mean his ghost hangs around while we go on living. I don't believe that. I wouldn't want him to hang around with us. He has much better things to be doing in Heaven. It must be so very interesting there. We don't know for sure that those in Heaven can see us, but we do know the martyrs there are waiting to see when this world will come to a conclusion. They are anxious, but they are told to rest until that time comes. (Rev. 6:10) What's important for us here now is knowing where are loved ones are, and being at peace with that. The more we can let them be there, the better we can get on with our lives here. That is what they would want for us. That, and to KNOW Jesus as our Savior.

I looked around at the green hills, the traffic, the other graves, and all I kept thinking was, he's not here.

I remember this moment so clearly. I don't believe these thoughts were coming from me. I believe this came from God. Our Father in Heaven doesn't want us mourning over these graves year after year. Yes, there is a time for that, of course. But after some time has passed, it is important to get our perspective right, and realize that these graves only contain the empty shells our loved ones lived in while they were here. It reminds me of the verse in Luke 24:5 (NIV), "Why do you look for the living among the dead?" Jesus had risen from the grave, *physically*. Our loved ones have not, but their spirits have, so they are not lying in those graves waiting. They are fully alive in Heaven. Even though we don't get our permanent new body until the return of Jesus, those in Heaven right now have a body that resembles their earthly body. People are able to recognize each other, no problem. Remember Moses and Elijah on the Mount of Transfiguration? (Matt. 17:1-9) There was no question who Jesus was talking to. We don't have all the answers for how it all works, but we have enough to know that we can trust God with every bit of it. And we do know, that on the day of Jesus' return, those buried in the ground will rise and be given a permanent new body. Then those who are still alive on that day will meet Jesus in the air—only the clothing and personal affects we are wearing will be left behind. In that moment, we will all be transformed! (1 Thessalonians 4:13-17)

After three days, Christ was no longer in His grave. He had conquered death. He had given us the Hope we all longed for—a way around what seemed and was so final.

I talked with a gentleman yesterday. His wife went Home to Heaven about eight months ago. He used the word *final*. He said the police came to his door. They said, "There is no easy way to tell you this. Your wife died in a car accident." (She actually had an embolism before the crash, so she was probably gone when the crash occurred. Thankfully, no one else was hurt.) I had to agree with him. It is SO final. And it is! But, it isn't. On this earth, yes, the finality is beyond human reasoning. But it is so good to know our eternity with God is so much more!

Even his dog knew something had happened. Shortly after Phil died, his dog Dackel jumped on his bed, went to his cheek to lick him, stopped, and turned around, and left before doing so.

Just sharing this again, it came to me; this was a gift from God. God used Dackel to help me comprehend what had happened. He showed me through her actions that Phil had truly left his body behind. What she couldn't express in words, God showed me by her actions. And she was deeply depressed for a year, and almost died herself. I don't understand all that, but I watched it happen. She, too, bounced back and found joy again. She lived a long and happy life, being later "adopted" by Phil's cousins.

Dearest friends, you were always so careful to follow my instructions when I was with you. And now that I am away you must be even more careful to put into action God's saving work in your lives, obeying God with deep reverence and fear. Philippians 2:12 (NLT)

This verse speaks to me of Phil being "away," and that I needed to be careful to put into action all the things we'd talked about through his long illness, especially during his last days. I try to be a person who is consistent. I don't like the saying, "Do what I say, not what I do." I wanted to be faithful to the things I taught Phil. I wanted to truly believe them. I wanted them to be true. By living them out and depending on God's way through the grief, I found out that it is all TRUE. God is faithful, and He does bind up the brokenhearted. I read recently, that when we believe in Jesus Christ as our Savior, *all* of the Holy Spirit comes to live inside of us. The question still remains, though, how much of us have we given *Him*? Have we given God **all** of our heart, soul and strength, so He has free reign in us to accomplish His work in and through us? God won't force Himself into our decisions; He is looking for willing participants.

It was comforting because so many of the memories that I had were foggy, and this brought them to light. It showed me that there were things said that needed to be said, that I had forgotten had been said.

This is IMPORTANT! We don't remember how it all went down. We think we do, but we are mistaken. Unless we write things down, and most don't, we will have misconceptions of things we said, didn't say, did, didn't do, etc... And because of that, we can be very hard on ourselves, or even on our loved ones who are gone. The best thing to do is to give ourselves a lot of grace, and everyone else, too. We all make mistakes—those that have gone on before us, and those of us who are still left here. Dwelling on those mistakes helps no one but the enemy, Satan. He wants us to live in misery. Let's throw that misery out with the trash, and allow God to help us remember the things that don't cause so much pain.

He said, "I just want us all to go together."

I remember Phil saying this, and it has always touched my heart. He knew he was leaving soon, but he didn't want to go alone. And, he didn't want those left to be hurting. I'm so glad we had these conversations, and that he felt free to share these thoughts with me. If I hadn't written them down, I may not have remembered them as I do, as I've stated before. So, as calculating as it may sound, maybe having a little notebook with us at someone's bedside would be a good idea. Don't we think we are always going to remember the cute things our kids say? I mean, who could ever forget them? And yet, we do.

He told me that he wished he had read more. Suddenly it all made sense to him.

Phil, like all of us, put many things in front of his time in the Word. Satan is so good at distracting us from God's love letters to us. While reading to Phil in his last days, it was like pouring God's sweet love right into his needful heart. It soothed him so. He said, "Mom, everything you're reading to me answers every question I have in my head." What an awesome tool God has given us to use in those most difficult moments. When I was reading to my friend, Barbara, who went Home to Heaven almost three years ago now, I thought she had gone to sleep, so I stopped reading. She quietly voiced the last word I had read, which was "eternal." I remember smiling, and continuing on, knowing she was still listening. She too felt God's sweet love being poured into her heart.

That is made easier when part of your heart already lives in Heaven with our Risen Lord. Believe me!

One foot in Heaven, the other foot on Earth. That's how a parent lives when they have a child in Heaven.

*The Cross is not foolishness to a dying boy, **or** to his parents!*

One day, when every knee does bow, the Cross will not be foolishness to anyone. I know our Father in Heaven would like all of us to take it seriously right now, right here, before His Son, Jesus, returns to take us Home. Why? Because, those who don't believe right here, right now, don't get to go. There is a literal Hell, and those who refuse God's gift of salvation will see that Hell one day. What a dreadful day that will be. Now is the time to give our hearts to Jesus. Not only does it help us every day we live on this earth, it will be our help for all of eternity

Gift #20 – The Cross of Jesus Christ becoming so real that we are more able to share its Hope with everyone we meet.

Is your pain being used as a mighty tool in God's Hand to bring you closer to Him?

Do you find the Scriptures more alive in your desperation? How so?

Record today's date and other notes you'd like to make:

The Great

<u>I AM</u>

Therefore, with minds that are alert and fully sober, set your hope on the grace to be brought to you when Jesus Christ is revealed at his coming.
1 Peter 1:13 (NIV)

CHAPTER TWENTY-ONE

"No eye has seen, no ear has heard,
and no mind has imagined
what God has prepared for those who love him."
1 Corinthians 2:9 (NLT)

Me

Can You Imagine?

Saturday, 06 Apr 2002

Have you ever imagined walking in my shoes? Taking yourself
through the years of chemo with your child and then saying good-
bye to them at the end? Have you? Do you know that you can't?
Your imaginings fall short of the reality of it. We can't walk in
another person's shoes. We can't know what they are really
feeling, or how difficult, or even how wonderful things really are
for them. Likewise, we can't imagine what Heaven will really be
like. But we can read about it, dream about it, and try to picture it.
But that's as far as we can get with it. Our thought process falls
short.

During my quiet time with God this morning, I realized that no matter how much Phil and I talked about what Heaven would be like, we could not come close to imagining what it would really be like until he saw it for himself; until we see it for ourselves.

I understood that better this morning when I thought about it in the context of others trying to understand what losing a child would feel like. If they allow their minds to even go there, it doesn't come close to what it's like. I know, because I have experienced both sides of that now—just as Phil has experienced both sides of thinking about Heaven, and actually experiencing Heaven.

*There were times when Phil was ill that I would let my mind wander down that road and try to imagine what life would be like without him; how I would feel. It was devastation. I would usually quickly retreat and start praying hard for his healing. The pain felt too great and the loss too large. And now, being on the other side of that fence, and living with the loss, there was no comparison. The feelings of devastation that were imagined were **minuscule** compared to the feelings of loss and devastation when it became a reality. Before Phil died, I could come back out of that thinking, back to praying for healing, and back to going wherever he was. I'd go and sit beside him and know that it was only my imaginings. Now I can't. Now I have to feel that devastation, and the only escape I have out of it is to trust in the One who took him Home. I have to know that he has not really died, but has gone on to a better place...a place I can't even imagine until I see it for myself. I just have to believe that Heaven is there, that he is there, and all that God has promised us is the Truth. I can do that. I am able to do that, because God makes me able.*

Jimm (son) said the other day that he always wondered how he would be if Phil should really die from this disease. He didn't know, and as he says now, he couldn't know until that time came. For him, he says it is easier than he thought it would be. Why? He says because for 5½ years, he didn't know where Phil was going. Now that he has become a Christian, which was shortly before

Phil died, he knows where Phil is. He knows that he will see him again, and he can rest in that.

"But we know these things because God has revealed them to us by his Spirit, and his Spirit searches out everything and shows us even God's deep secrets."
1 Corinthians 2:10 (NLT)

Jimm knows now because he has not only experienced the death of his brother, but he also believes in God and the resurrection of Jesus Christ. God has revealed these things to him. He knows the Truth because he has God's Spirit living in him now. He took that step of faith.

"No one can know what anyone else is really thinking except that person alone, and no one can know God's thoughts except God's own Spirit. And God has actually given us his Spirit so we can know the wonderful things God has freely given us."
1 Corinthians 2:11 (NLT)

*I am glad that you can't really know this feeling of loss, because the reality of it is so hard. I don't want you to have to feel it, and I don't really even want you to try and imagine what it might be like. I don't, because I have, and now I know, and I don't wish this upon anyone. I'd rather you stay where you are, deal with your own things, and leave this one for us to deal with in the way that God is teaching us to. There's no need to go there. I'm not saying don't pray for us, and don't encourage us. NO, NO, NO. That's not what I'm saying. We need your help, and your encouragement, and your prayers. That's God's love pouring through you into us. I just don't want you to do that by trying to imagine what it's like to walk in our shoes. That's not necessary. You have your own things to deal with in this life. But, I **would** like you to try and imagine Heaven, or wherever you're headed, because that is something you should think about. God has prepared a place for those who love Him, and we should think about that place. I long for that place, where tears will be wiped away. I want to know Jesus, and I want Him to know me. When He comes back, I want it to be like my Best Friend* *has just arrived. I can't wait to greet Him and tell Him how glad I am that He has come. I want us to know each other so well that there is no question that where Jesus goes, I will follow!*

How do I do that? How do I get to know Jesus that well? How am I assured of that at our meeting? By spending time with Jesus in the Word and in prayer, for sure. But I think, mostly by, stopping the "doing," and just focusing on Him throughout the day.

"As you enter the house of God, keep your ears open and your mouth shut! Don't be a fool who doesn't realize that mindless offerings to God are evil." Ecclesiastes 5:1 (NLT)

Verse 3
Just as being too busy gives you nightmares, being a fool makes you a blabbermouth.

Working hard is not a bad thing. Don't get me wrong. There are a lot of things for us to do here for the Kingdom of God. I love writing e-mails and working for the Master, but He wants us to love Him first and foremost. If our child turns their back on us, won't have anything to do with us, wants no relationship with us, and won't spend time in their day with us, but has time to mow the lawn, wash the car, and take out the garbage without fail, how would we feel? Wouldn't we want them to sit down for a moment and spend some time with us? I think I would, as much as I would have loved it if the boys would have done all those chores without question. I know it would not have taken very long before I noticed that the chores were getting done, but the relationship was sour.

"Be silent before the Lord, all humanity, for he is springing into action from his holy dwelling." Zechariah 2:13 (NLT)

*I can't do this, but God can. I need to be silent before Him. As much as I would like to move right through this whole grief process in about 2.5 months, that is not to be. It **is a process** and it is controlled by God, as is everything. My job is to grow closer to Him, to know Him more and more, and the rest will happen in*

God's timing. There are days when the pain is removed from my heart, and I feel light, easy, and oh so good. There are days when I wake with a heavy heart and carry it through my day, only wanting to go to bed early that night because the weight of it has worn me down. It is good to know that I am not even in control of my own emotions. God is. He will also be the one to take this grief from my heart. It is nothing I can do on my own. I have tried, and when I stop trying, God shows me how simple it can be by just loving Him and knowing Him.

I thank God for the good days and draw close to Him. I ask for help from God on the bad days, and draw close to Him. There is a light at the end of this dark tunnel and that light grows larger as the days go on. It is a light of Hope for the days here on this earth, and also a light of Hope of a place that I cannot even imagine. It's a place where Phil now lives. He no longer needs to just imagine. I want to be still, know God, and trust Him to heal my broken heart.

Love, Diane

Myself

Have you ever imagined walking in my shoes?

I know we do that. We try to imagine another person's pain. It really is good to not be able to fully "go there" for each other, so that we can "be there" for each other, offering comfort. Just this morning in reading a devotional, it talked about the dark valleys we all have to go through. No one escapes this life without them. But as I read about that, and thought about how the author talked about the value in those dark valleys, I thought about how we can **read** that, but do we really **believe** that? Do we believe dark valleys really work for our benefit? *Before* we enter into them, I don't think we can comprehend that thoroughly. *While* we are in the dark valleys, we question their worth. I believe, it's only in the coming *out of* them with God's powerful love at work, that we can begin to understand their value. And it's not that we would wish that long dark valley on anyone, nor would we have chosen it. But these experiences do allow us the opportunity, should we choose it, to then be an asset for others who are coming along behind us in their own trials.

*The feelings of devastation that were imagined were **minuscule** compared to the feelings of loss and devastation when it became a reality. Before Phil died, I could come back out of that thinking.*

That was always a relief, to be able to go and put my arms around Phil, and take him out for a cheeseburger and try to forget how horrible it all was. It is true; God gives us just enough manna for each day to survive, just like He did the Israelites. "Our ancestors ate the manna in the wilderness; as it is written: 'He gave them bread from heaven to eat.'" (John 6:31) At that point, when Phil was still with us on this earth, I had just the right amount of nourishment from God. If God had given me enough manna to survive living without Phil before he actually left us, it would have overflowed the "barns." It wasn't needed. I needed to just stay on the day we were on, take in what God was giving me, and work with what was happening then. God surely knows.

But I just have to believe that Heaven is there, that he is there, and all that God has promised us is the Truth.

I wrote this when Phil was just gone months. Phil has been gone YEARS now, and this is still so very true! This is where my mind MUST stay so I can keep putting one foot in front of the other. It does get easier with practice. But just like muscles that will get out of condition if we stop exercising, it is still important to stay closely connected to God each day. Recently, I read something like this: "One day without the Word, and I notice. Two days without the Word, and my family notices. Three days without the Word, and the world notices." This is very true in the grief walk. Without being plugged in daily to the Truth, the enemy will come with his army of lies and invade any vulnerable territory we will give him.

We need your help, and your encouragement, and your prayers. That's God's love pouring through you into us.

The Church is the Body of Christ. Every part is needed. I have a friend right now who is missing her sister who went Home to Heaven a few weeks back. This same friend poured into my life when I was hurting. I am now able to pour into hers. That is how it works. If we try to make it alone, without others, and without God, we will fail. It is assured. Don't even try it. Plug into the Body, and stay plugged into God. One day, you will be the source of Hope for someone else!

God has prepared a place for those who love Him, and we should think about that place.

Many have said this through the centuries, and maybe many will be saying it in future centuries, but I'm saying it right now, "Be ready to meet Jesus!" We need to be prepared to meet our Savior. He will be coming back one day, and even if it isn't in our lifetime, that's all the more reason to be prepared, because we will be going to meet with Him. Jesus may not be coming in our next heartbeat, but we are all only one heartbeat away from meeting Him. Thinking about what has been prepared for us in Heaven is a wonderful thought in this treacherous world. I watched a movie the other day, and sitting there I thought, "This life is so hard on so many." It is. If you are reading this book, it's probably because life has been hard on you too. But it is not impossible to live this life joyfully when we have Jesus. Yes, there will be down times. But there can also be many, many, many up times! Watch for those. Live in those for as long as possible, and always give thanks for all things.

How do I get to know Jesus that well?

Jesus wants to be our Best Friend. Isn't that inviting? When we know someone wants to be friends with us, it makes it so much easier to be around them, getting to know them. If we feel like we have to force our way into the Throne Room of God, that's not a very warm welcome. But we don't have to force ourselves. Ephesians 3:12 (NLT) says, "…we can come fearlessly into God's presence, assured of his glad welcome." Jesus is there at the right hand of the Father. He is happy to meet with us. It is there that we will get to know Him. Starting in the Word, we can read, pray, and spend time learning about all the things of Heaven. If you want to read an excellent book about Heaven, I'd recommend the one by Randy Alcorn, simply called, "Heaven." You may be surprised at all the Bible contains about our future Home, and what our Best Friend has waiting for us!

It is good to know that I am not even in control of my own emotions. God is. He will also be the one to take this grief from my heart. It is nothing I can do on my own.

It's interesting reading that. It makes me wonder why some days can be so good, and others so hard. Our flesh, our mind, and our emotions are very complex. I can be sitting in the very same chair one minute as happy as can be. And in the next moment, feel completely different, and not one thing has changed. Are we to trust such emotions, such thoughts, and such fleshy reactions to the world around us? It seems not. But God never, ever changes! We can run to Him on good days and bad. He is there for us. The more we get to know that, the more we can ignore what our flesh, mind, and emotions are putting us through!

There is a light at the end of this dark tunnel and that light grows larger as the days go on.

This book is titled, *It Started in the Dark*. Why? Because 12 years ago was a dark time, both emotionally and as a writer. That Light 12 years ago, was a dim flicker of Hope many years down the road. Sometimes I knew it was there, sometimes I just hoped it was while I clung to the Hope we have in Jesus with all my might. Today, I live in that Light, and in that Hope! And the Light just keeps getting brighter. When it seems all healing is finished, God still brings new things into my life to show me that He is still working on this process. I just went skiing for the first time in 16 years. (Author's picture was taken on that trip.) I gave up what I loved for someone that I love, because Phil needed me to be able to take care of him. My broken bones would not have been in his best interest. He needed a Mom who was available to care for him. There are still things, like skiing, that are coming back into my life. There have been layers of life that have been affected that I never even knew were there, but God knew. And God cares about them all. We have to keep embracing every bit and parcel of His healing. When we do, we will see that we serve an amazing God!

Gift #21 – The gift of more healing when we didn't even realize what needed tending to.

What large or small piece of healing have you received recently?

Were you aware of that area of your life that God needed to touch?

Record today's date and other notes you'd like to make:

The Great

<u>I AM</u>

Be silent before the Lord, all humanity, for he is springing into action from his holy dwelling.
Zechariah 2:13 (NLT)

CHAPTER TWENTY-TWO

"And be sure of this: I am with you always,
even to the end of the age."
Matthew 28:20b (NLT)

<u>Me</u>

Watch Closely...God at Work!

Wednesday, 17 Apr 2002

Where was God? Where was God on 9-11? Where was God the night Phil died? Where is He now? God, that is? Don't a lot of people ask that question? Don't we all at times?

So where is He?

Isaiah 65:1-3 (NIV)
"I revealed myself to those who did not ask for me; I was found by those who did not seek me. To a nation that did not call on my name, I said, 'Here am I, here am I.' All day long I have held out my hands to an obstinate people, who walk in ways not good,

pursuing their own imaginations—a people who continually provoke me to my very face."

God is here! He has always been here, and He will always be here. Are we looking for Him? Are we seeking Him? Are we calling on His name? Are we pursuing Him, or just our own plans and dreams? Did you know that He can be found even when we are not seeking Him? This verse made me think about that. Before I became a Christian, I'm not sure that I was seeking God. I think I was a little interested, although I would not admit it. I think I wanted God, but if you'd asked me, I would have said I didn't. And I would have said, "Don't talk to me about it." What was that?... Yes, I was actually listening. But I would have acted like I wasn't.

I know it was God calling to me, revealing Himself to me before I even knew I longed for Him. He was there all the time. I just didn't know it. I was obstinate, proud, living my own life. Why would I need God? But I did then, and I do now, more than ever.

And where was God on the night Phil died? He was right here, with us, in more ways than I even realized, taking care of things I might never have noticed. But the more I grow and learn about God, the more He reveals how He cares for us, even when we aren't paying a lot of attention. He helps us even before we are grateful for His help, because He loves us that much. God doesn't require a "Thank You." But I'm sure He's happy when He gets one. He doesn't even require an acknowledgment. But I'm sure He's happy when we notice Him. He doesn't ask anything of us except that we love Him. So many don't love God. But even so, He doesn't wait until we honor Him before He's willing to help us, and be there for us. We may ignore Him our whole lives, right up until the day we die, and God won't force us to love Him. Only AFTER we have taken our last breath have we lost Him completely. But then, when we see Him on our last day, every knee will bow. He won't force us to bow, we will do so automatically because of who He is. The choice will be a non-issue. God is God, and there will be no doubt about it. There will be no more doubts. There won't be a "Doubting Thomas" in Heaven. We will see the nail scars in

Jesus' hands and feet. But our time of decision making will have ended. The believers and non-believers will be separated for all of eternity, and the time of God's full glory being revealed will have begun.

So, what do we do here on earth before that day comes? How do we find God in this crazy world we live in? In the trials and tribulations that come into our lives, and even the happy and wonderful days in our lives? How do we see God when prayers seem unanswered, and children die? When planes crash, wars are fought, and people are starving? I think we see Him in all the little things that so many times go unnoticed. They go unnoticed only because we are not watching for them. We are not looking for God. We are distracted by the world, and missing out on all that our Lord is doing for us, around us, and through us.

*This became clearer the other day when I was, once again, being attacked by the evil one. Yes, the devil. He does exist! He started attacking me once again with all the things that I should have done the night Phil died—the things I should have said. The "How could you's?", and the "What kind of mother are you anyway?", type of thoughts. Thoughts that will **destroy** a person if they are allowed to remain.*

I prayed to God for help once again, as these thoughts, this battle, in my mind raged. As I prayed, God swooped in and asked me to take another look at that last evening, from His point of view. Now, I know some of you are probably wondering just how God does that. That's a difficult one to explain. Prayer, and the way God fights our spiritual battles for us, is a wonderful thing. Most of it is done in our very own minds and understanding this Scripture.

"But you belong to God, my dear children. You have already won your fight with these false prophets, because the Spirit who lives in you is greater than the spirit who lives in the world."
1 John 4:4 (NLT)

So there I was, being filled with all these terrible thoughts about that last night, and God says, "Whoa! Look at it this way," so to speak. The Holy Spirit was working within me. The "conversation" went like this:

The devil's lies and deceptions: "How could you just go to sleep next to Phil that night, knowing he might not wake up in the morning? Why did you not wrap your arms around him, tell him how much you loved him and would miss him? What kind of mother are you?"

God: "Remember the prayer you prayed that last day? You told me that you didn't know how long this would go on, whether it would be a day, or a month, or perhaps Phil would have total healing and not be going Home at all? But you asked Me to give you strength to remain by Phil's bedside for as long as was needed."

Me: "Oh, yeah, I remember that. Even though others might have clearly seen that Phil was dying, as his mother, I didn't really know that. It was probably a protective fog that You placed around me, giving me peace that transcends understanding, during that difficult time. And I did wrap my arms around Phil. I tried to warm his body as it seemed to shiver from cold. But he asked me not to. He said I was too heavy. It was probably because he was trying to leave, and how could he if I was wrapped around him?"

The devil: "How could you just sit there by his bed, calmly holding his hand that day? Your child was dying. Why weren't you fighting this terrible disease? Why weren't you pouring more chemo into his body? Don't you love your son? Why weren't you fighting?!"

God: "Remember when you prayed for direction and lightning bolts to know My will for further treatment for Phil? Remember those 'lightning bolts' I sent, and the peace you felt when you made the decision, along with Jim and Phil, that the chemo would be stopped? Remember that Phil almost died at that time? But when you sought My direction and took that step of faith, Phil started feeling so much better, and enjoyed more than a year of life without chemo."

Me: "Yes, I remember. I remember that sense of peace when the decision was made and how before we even discussed it with Phil, he got up the next morning feeling better. And how we talked with him about it while sitting at McDonald's that day. I told him we were going to stop the chemo, and he was so happy. I then told him that it meant he might have only three months without chemo, but he could have maybe a year with it. I asked him what he would like to do. He said he'd like the three months without chemo. And when he prayed about it, he also felt God was telling him to stop the chemo."

The devil: "But where was God the night Phil died?"

God: "Remember. Where was I? I was with you, in Phil's room. Remember when Phil's breathing was so loud, and you thought you should maybe give him a pill to calm him down? You got up out of his bed to go and get him a drink of water. When you went to the door, Chris was standing right there. Who brought him to the door right at that moment? I did. Phil had been breathing loudly for almost two hours, but Chris was right there at that very moment. What made Chris even stay home that night when he always went out in the evening? What brought him to Phil's door just as you stepped outside of it so that you could ask him to go and get that drink of water? And who changed your mind right then—because you didn't ask him for the drink of water did you? But instead you said to him, 'Chris, go get Dad.' Why did you say that? Then as you turned and went back into Phil's room, what happened? What did Phil say to you? What would you have missed had you left his room?"

Me: "Phil said, 'Mom, I think God is healing me. I'm really feeling a lot better. I'm going to feel good tomorrow, Mom.' And I said, 'I love you, Phil.' And he said, 'I love you, Mom.'"

God: "Why do you think that was?"

Me: "Because You wanted those to be the last words we spoke to each other."

*God: "And I kept you in his room because I didn't want you to miss Phil's healing before he left this earth. And I wanted you to be with him like you had requested. And I wanted Jim and Chris to be there, too. So I kept Chris home that night and had him there to go get Jim for you. And then I took Phil Home, painlessly, and feeling better than he had felt in 5½ years. I was there. **I was there!** I'm **always** there with you!"*

Me: "You were there every second, God, and I see You so clearly now that You have reminded me of these things. Your timing was perfect. Your plan was perfect. Your love surrounded us, and it always will."

The devil: …………………………………(Nothing but silence.)

Me: Deep breath...the devil is gone...the lies have stopped for now.

God's Word: *"This is what the Lord says: Do not be afraid! Don't be discouraged by this mighty army, for the battle is not yours, but God's." 2 Chronicles 20:15 (NLT)*

Sometimes we know God is with us, and sometimes He is busy at work when we think we are on our own. Sometimes it's not until later, that things are revealed, that His goodness and care for us shines through. The devil would like to torture us and make us believe that God has deserted us in our times of great trouble. But if we look closely, we will see the hand of God on all things, especially during those difficult times. It's during those times, when we don't really have time to think, or time to make decisions, or call the shots—and emotions and stakes are running so high— that God is most active. I think, it is during those times that God's protective fog shields us from what the enemy would like to do, and God helps us do what needs to be done.

*I wasn't thinking clearly the last few days of Phil's life. I was living through a time when it would have been impossible, without God, to put one foot in front of the other as I watched my child in his bed dying from Leukemia. I did silly things like the laundry. I remember putting the clothes in Phil's drawer and telling him, "See Phil, I'm doing your laundry, and I'm not even crying. God is going to take care of us like He always has." (We're going to be fine.) Only with the strength of God could a mother say something like that to her dying child. Phil needed to be reassured that it was okay to leave us behind. He **needed** that, and God **provided** that.*

God provides, God watches over, and God answers our prayers. It is in His timing, and in His way. God's way is perfect. I know that. I have seen that!

***Don't listen to the lies.** They will only take you down and destroy you. They have almost destroyed me at times. But when I call out to God, He rescues me, and He will continue to do so.*

These "conversations" with the devil and God go on daily in my life, as they probably do in yours. It doesn't take something this catastrophic to be caught up in the lies and deceptions that the evil one would like to destroy us with. The devil wants us to think that God is not in control, that things are chaotic, and there is no order to this world. But there is perfect order to this world, and one day we will see that. Until then, we just have to trust that it is so. But we can also witness some of it, if we are watching God work.

Watch closely. God is a joy to behold.

Have a great day.

Love, Diane

Myself

And where was God on the night Phil died? He was right here, with us, in more ways than I even realized, taking care of things I might never have noticed.

Hindsight is 20/20 they say. It's like the verse in the Bible about the Lord hiding Moses in the cleft of the rock so that all His glory could pass by. Only after He had passed by, could Moses see what God had done. I was with my friend, Aimee, the other day and she was buying a gift for a priest/friend who was turning 70. When we saw a Cross with "Rock of Ages" on it, it struck me as the perfect gift for him. When a man, and especially a priest who has lived in the Word, turns 70, there is much hindsight, much godly wisdom that has been gained through the years. It can be a time of looking back, gleaning from lessons learned, and then passing them on to future generations.

But what do we do here on earth before that day comes? How do we find God in this crazy world we live in? In the trials and tribulations that come into our lives, and even the happy and wonderful days in our lives?

I think this answer is found in the paragraph above. How do we live in the turmoil, having not lived through it before? We attach ourselves to people who have lived a good many years. We attach ourselves to people who know the Lord through thick and thin. My brother, Steve, knows the Word so well. When I talk with him, I know I will hear Scripture spoken, guaranteed. When we sit with people who know Jesus, like Mary sitting at Jesus' feet, we will glean from them as they talk about the things of God. This is true fellowship. In this way we can be encouraged and warned, just as the Word tells us we ought to be.

How do we see God when prayers seem unanswered, and children die? When planes crash, and wars are fought? When people are starving?

We all long to see God, and we all long for there to come a day when bad things don't happen. That's when we have to focus our eyes on eternity by setting our sights on things of Heaven, and not just the things of this world. I read recently that speaking of this *world*, and speaking of this *earth*, are two very different things. The earth is God's, and everything in it and on it. But this world is fallen because of what happened in the garden. This world gets uglier and uglier with the choices that are being made and as the day of Jesus coming back for His Church draws nigh. But this earth, even though it reaps what man has sown down through the ages, can still show us so many beautiful aspects of our Creator. His creation shouts His name! His ocean waves, smells of pine, sunsets, and waterfalls can give us glimpses of how things ought to be. We can sit still, and soak our Lord in, even as the world falls apart around us.

Only with the strength of God could a mother say something like that to her dying child. Phil needed to be reassured that it was okay to leave us behind. He needed that, and God provided that.

Once again, I breathe in deep as I read that, and I wonder how in the world...okay, there is that word. *World.* So it is not "how in the *world*," because in the world's system, that is not possible. But it is how in the power of the *Holy Spirit*, that we must live out each day. Times like this are supernatural. And upon looking back, we can start to take notice of that. If I had looked ahead before those final days, and tried to figure out how I was going to walk this out with Phil—if I had tried to play it all out in my mind—it would have never played out like this. Doing laundry? Even as I read this today, I think about how crazy that was. But then again, as I sit here on this day, I know now how NEEDED that was. If I just sat by Phil's bed crying and worrying, he would have been crying and worrying along with me. What kind of faith would that have looked like to him? But if I could do some of the "normal" things of life, while still caring for him, then I believe that was exactly what he needed to see. He wanted to go Home towards the end, but he needed to be encouraged to do just that. He was smart enough and old enough to know, that his leaving was not going to be an easy thing for those that loved him. God helped us help him leave. And I am grateful.

It's during those times, when we don't really have time to think, or time to make decisions, or call the shots—when emotions and stakes are running so high—that God is most active.

This really came to light for me just recently. I had a big event coming up in our family, and I knew there could be some challenging things going on. I spent time praying that morning, getting ready. When the time came, and difficult situations arose, I didn't have to run to my Bible and seek direction. The direction was already planted in me, I just had to listen to the Holy Spirit and follow His moment-by-moment directions. It's like I read recently about making prayer deposits in the morning, because we will need to be writing spiritual checks later in the day. We don't want those "checks" bouncing all over the place. We need to have enough in the "bank" to cover them. We NEVER know what any day holds; but we can know Who holds it. And when we start our days in God's presence by being in His Word, He will see us through whatever challenges come our way.

These "conversations" with the devil and God go on daily in my life.

Isaiah 65:3 at the start of this chapter ends with: *"...people who continually provoke me to my very face."* How many of us have experienced being provoked by others, directly to our face, and/or being provoked by our own thoughts that come from a dark place? But how many of us realize that this is not a battle between flesh and blood, but a spiritual battle in an unseen world? In Ephesians 6:10-18 it talks about this battle, and about putting on the full armor of God. It says we are to use every piece of God's armor to resist the enemy, so that after the battle we will be standing firm. This doesn't say "if" there is a battle, it says "after" the battle. God knows the battles will come in our lives. And He warns us about them, and tells us how to be ready for them. God KNOWS what He is talking about. He knows the enemy we fight daily. He hears the lies that are being told to us. And our Father in Heaven is telling us not to believe them, to resist them, and to use His armor to do this. He says, "Put on My armor!" And we need to DAILY. When we are grieving, the battle is fierce for our mind, our will, and our emotions. The ONLY way to win is to let God fight the lies for us as we stand within His armor and protection.

Gift #22 – Learning to resist the enemy and the forces he brings against us through God's power and protection!

What lies have you been hearing lately?

What choices are you making in resisting what the enemy is trying to do to you?

Record today's date and other notes you'd like to make:

The Great

<u>I AM</u>

When my glory passes by, I will put
you in a cleft in the rock and cover
you with my hand until I have passed by.
Exodus 33:22 (NIV)

CHAPTER TWENTY-THREE

*There is a time for everything, a season
for every activity under heaven.*
Ecclesiastes 3:1 (NLT)

<u>Me</u>

Spider-Man

Monday, 06 May 2002

*It's May. "Spider-Man" has been released. I knew it was coming;
all who like movies knew it was coming. Phil knew it was coming.
He saw the posters. He saw the release date. He knew...and he
knew there was a very strong possibility that he would not be here
to see the movie. What a strange thought for a young boy who
should have about 70 years ahead of him, to think he might not be
here in seven months. I sometimes wonder what was going through
his mind, even though we were able to talk about so many things.
I'm sure there were things he kept to himself for privacy sake, and
to save his mother the heartache and tears. I know I had thoughts
that I did not share with him for the very same reasons.*

He had to know that if he was not here when "Spider-Man" was released, it would hurt those left behind. I know he was disappointed thinking he might miss it. When Phil turned 16, his last birthday and just a month before he died, he received a silky Spider-Man shirt that he really liked. Also, about a month before Phil died, I was finishing up a pencil drawing of Spider-Man swinging over some villain. We went together to pick out the frame, not something Phil normally enjoyed doing, but this was for a special picture that would hang in his room. It's in there now, on his wall. His shirt is hanging in his closet.

What's a mother to do with all of this? Cry, for sure, and pray for peace. I also avoid. I don't want to see the movie. I don't want to see the ads. I don't want to see the toys released, or the cereal, or the clothing. I don't want to, but it will surround me. Everyone is talking about the movie, as is to be expected. I can't really avoid it, although I try. Jim saw the movie on Friday; the day it was released. That was his way of honoring Phil. I did not see it. I won't. That is the choice I am making. I don't need the added heartache. It hurts enough already. I'd like to bury my head in the sand until it leaves the theaters. But I can't. In fact, I may go to the show tomorrow and see another movie. For some reason I just feel like going. Maybe it's God urging me to take another step in healing. He is not asking me to go to see "Spider-Man," but maybe He is asking me to face the pain, at least halfway. God doesn't want me to avoid things because they hurt. I believe He wants me to work through them with His help. He doesn't call me to step into the middle of the fire, but perhaps He calls me to step up close and get used to the heat. Because, there will always be "heat." There will always be memories that cause me pain, there will always be places that are difficult to go to, and there will always be talk that I would rather avoid. These things could cause me to be a prisoner in my grief. Little by little, God will ask me to step closer, breathe deeply, and trust Him to see me through all of it.

Phil collected state quarters. He put them in a board that his Bedstemor (Grandma) gave him. He enjoyed when each new one would come out, placing it proudly in his map of the U.S. The quarters still come out every so often, just as they did before he died. Now, I don't like that. I don't like that he won't be here to see his map completed. But he probably knew that also. I surely thought about it. Will he be here to complete this picture? Now, I just set the new quarters on his dresser. I step close to the heat, but not right into it. I don't want to place them in his U.S. map. I don't want to; not yet. It hurts way too much. I have enough pain. Why add to it? In time, and there will come a time, I will. There will come a time for all things. But God is not in a hurry, and I don't want to be either. In time, with God's help, I will work through all these things. The pain will lessen, and the memories will become more cherished...in time.

Ecclesiastes 3:1-5 (NLT)
There is a time for everything, a season for every activity under heaven.
A time to be born and a time to die.
A time to plant and a time to harvest.
A time to kill and a time to heal.
A time to tear down and a time to rebuild
A time to cry and a time to laugh.
A time to grieve and a time to dance.
A time to scatter stones and a time to gather stones.
A time to embrace and a time to turn away.

I just got home from a women's retreat with my church. We went to the beautiful Hayes Mansion down in San Jose. Last year I gave a short testimony and talked about Phil. We had just gotten back from Hawaii with the boys. Phil spent the weekend with my parents. This year, it was so strange to be there and not have him to come home to. But you know what? I had a great time on this retreat. And I am so grateful for that. I don't take that for granted at all these days. There were many times over the weekend when I would stop in my thoughts and think, "I'm really having a good time." I'd thank God.

It must be that there's time for some of that, in God's timing, because I certainly don't have the ability to make that decision. It is a gift from Him that comes unexpectedly. Like when I was out to *lunch a couple of weeks ago with some friends—we laughed, and joked, and talked, and suddenly, I realized I was having FUN; actual fun, and with no pain in my heart. I didn't notice that the pasta I was eating was Phil's favorite, or that the street the restaurant was on was the one we had walked down together, or anything like that. I did spot a picnic table as I was parking my car that Phil and I had had lunch at not so long ago, but that thought came and went quickly. Was this any of my doing? No, it was all part of God's healing. Little by little, I will laugh easily again. I will have stepped close to the "heat" and not gotten burned so badly so as to not want to return. I will find out that I can survive this pain, that God will remove this pain in His timing, and I will live fully again...in time.*

Do I want it now? YES! I want this pain to go away almost as much as I want Phil back. One of these I will eventually come close to; the other, I will have to wait until I leave this earth myself.

Our speaker this weekend was a wonderful woman. She shared briefly about the loss of her son eight years ago. I later found out that Friday night was her son's birthday. We didn't know that as she stood and shared God's Word with us. We didn't know the pain she felt in her heart or the memories that filled her thinking. All we knew was that she stood teaching us about God's grace that night. Do I draw inspiration from women like this? You bet I do! I believe one of our jobs here is to encourage each other in this world. In this life that can be so difficult. There was not one woman in that room who did not have something in her life that caused her pain of some sort, whether it was her marriage, her children, her past, or maybe what she thought her future held. And when our speaker can stand up there and share the Word of God with confidence and talk about God's sustaining love after what she has gone through, she inspires us all!

By the way, I just said that I want Phil back. This is not entirely true. Of course I do, but I don't. And I was happy to have a talk with our speaker, and she said to me that she would not want her son to have to come back into this world after experiencing Heaven. I thanked her for sharing that with me, because I told her that I agree with her. I wouldn't want Phil to have to leave Heaven after being there, no matter what pain I feel with missing him.

This pain molds me, shapes me, and refines me—and most importantly, it draws me closer to God each day. I don't have the luxury of putting God on the back burner until I'm ready for Him. I'm ready for Him all the time, because without Him, life doesn't make a whole lot of sense.

As our speaker shared about her son, I knew many in the audience felt the same pain and were missing their children. Then the worship leader got up to lead us in more singing and she shared the loss of her five year old and a baby. It almost got to be too much. I know some women were growing uncomfortable. They started thinking if this could happen to so many around me, what about me? That's a thought we don't like to think about, because these things always happen to the "other guy." But you know what? They don't. And when it happens to you, it causes you to have strange thoughts—like when I was pumping gas into my car the other day, watching all the other cars drive by. I thought, "None of you will be here in 100 years, unless you're probably two or less." How many people think thoughts like that as they fill their cars with gas? Yes, I admit it's strange, but it's only because I see life from a different perspective now. We all think we're going to live forever, because most of us don't even think about dying until we're faced with it. How sad is that? Sadder I think than mourning Phil. Want to know why? Because, if we only focus on living here on earth, we miss out on really living as we are called to. How's that? Because with our focus on this world, we stress about this world, and we miss the whole point of what we're even doing here, and why God created us.

I used to think deathbed conversions were so unfair. People lived their whole lives and didn't have to obey God at all. They just confessed their sins, accepted Christ, and went right on to Heaven, having done exactly what they wanted for their whole lives. Now, I *think just the opposite. I think about all that they **missed** out on by not knowing God their entire lives. Because **true joy** is found in knowing and following Jesus, not in just living this life however we please. But that's a mystery you only discover after you've taken that step of faith.*

Will the tragedy of losing a child happen to you? Probably not. But something will happen to everyone; we are guaranteed of that. "I have told you all this so that you may have peace in me. Here on earth you will have many trials and sorrows. But take heart, because I have overcome the world." John 16:33 (NLT)

Everyone will have trials and tribulations of one kind or another. This is not said to depress you, but to encourage you, because believers can take heart. Jesus has overcome the world. We have Hope. With Hope in eternity, this life, with its fleeting problems, diminishes. Trials and tribulations can't destroy us. The worst thing of all, death, has lost its sting! If God is for us, who can be against us?

You may think this is a strange thing to say, but do you know that it is a privilege for me to have had Phil, and to have had to say good-bye to Phil? Because I know in the future, when my heart is healed, I will be able to help others who see no Hope in their sorrows. This trial has left me with a passion to help others in similar situations. I never would have had that otherwise. I hope to be able to encourage others and to help them see that Jesus heals the brokenhearted. I hope to come alongside others, share my pain and joy, and hopefully show them with God, all things are possible. By comforting them, I will also be comforted.

Yes, Phil changed my life, for the better, just by being here. Because of him, life makes more sense. His life has helped me focus my life on God. God has taught me how important it is to be there for others, to encourage them through any trial, and to patiently endure all this world can throw at us. This world is temporary. It is only the first step in our long walk to eternity. You will spend eternity somewhere, do you know that? Where will you be? Hell won't be the party you're looking for. The feasting will be done in Heaven with the King. That's where I want to be!

In 100 years, our choice will have been made and secured; maybe even sooner, if Jesus comes back for us before then. In 100 years, we won't be here, that's guaranteed. We don't know what tomorrow holds, or what we will have to endure. But we can know where our Hope lies, and where we will spend eternity.

"Spider-Man" won't matter in Heaven. State quarters won't matter in Heaven. And all these tears will be a thing of the past. That's Hope I **can** *and* **do** *hang on to!*

Thank you for letting me share my broken heart with you. It helps to release these emotions that need to be released, and move on down the road just a bit more.

Love,
Diane

Myself

What's a mother to do with all of this? Cry, for sure, and pray for peace. I also avoid. I don't want to see the movie.

Twelve years later, and I still have not seen the movie. I haven't seen Spider-Man I, II, or III, or however many they have made. Jim has seen them all, and enjoys them. It's not that I can't at this point, it's that I don't out of a strange loyalty to Phil. I don't think it comes out of brokenness as much as stubbornness. If he can't see them, then I won't either. But I never know what tomorrow holds —and we don't know for sure what Heaven holds for us concerning this. Maybe there are movies and entertainment there beyond our wildest imagination. Spider-Man can't rival Jesus!

Jim saw the movie on Friday; the day it was released. That was his way of honoring Phil.

Jim does honor Phil's memory this way. And that says a lot. He walks into the pain, and grows through it. It is also a good thing to think about, that all people grieve differently. There is no right or wrong. The only thing that we need to focus on is, what is most honoring to the person, and to our God? Jim never tells me I should see the movies, and I never tell him he shouldn't. We have given each other a lot of understanding and love through each challenge we have faced.

Maybe it's God urging me to take another step in healing. He is not asking me to go to see "Spider-Man." But maybe He is asking me to face the pain, at least halfway.

Phil and I went to a lot of movies together. We did a lot of things together, since he was out of school so much of the time. Each time I did something new, that we had done together, it caused me pain. But each time I did it after that, the pain lessened a little bit. It got to the point where I would think about it, and then notice that the pain wasn't there. And then it got to the point where I didn't think about it at all a lot of the time. I just went and did the things we used to, walking in the new normal of him not being with me. It is a process that we must walk through and out of.

God doesn't want me to avoid things because they hurt. I believe He wants me to work through them with His help.

God is asking all of us to do things that are VERY difficult. But He is not asking us to do things that are impossible. All things are possible through Christ who strengthens us. That is a promise in the Bible. It is a promise we will believe after we have experienced it. We have to walk it out for it to become real to us. That is the hard part. That is the walk of faith. Eventually on that walk, God's promises will penetrate into our hearts and heal them. I was truly hoping that would be true for me. I found that they are!

These things could cause me to be a prisoner in my grief.

Grief can be like a jail cell—the door slams shut, the bars echo of emptiness, and the light seems to be but a dim bulb over in the corner somewhere. We can choose to go and sit in the darkness, or we can stand under that dim bulb with our Bible opened up, and start to read, read, read—and pray, pray, pray. Those are our choices. Otherwise, grief will swallow us up.

The pain will lessen, and the memories will become more cherished...in time.

And just as in the paragraphs above, the reading, the praying, and the walking it out in faith will bring us into the freedom that belongs to us in Christ. No other "religion" on this earth promises us what Jesus does. That's because Jesus isn't a religion; He is our Friend and Savior. Jesus is like a breath of fresh air when we are with Him. He guides us and leads us, and helps us get that key that's dangling outside of the jail cell, over by the dog, wagging its tail. (Those of you who have been on the Pirates of the Caribbean ride at Disneyland will understand what I'm saying there.) Jesus will unlock our cell, and bring us out into the light of day again. Remember how Paul and Silas sang praises in their cell, and their chains fell off, and the prison doors opened?! It's still happening today in the hearts of those who sing God's praises!! (Acts 16:25-34)

Was this any of my doing? No, it was all part of God's healing. Little by little, I will laugh easily again.

The great thing about the Holy Spirit is, He works in us in the gentlest of ways, and usually we have to look back to have noticed what He has been doing! But we MUST look back, and take notice! Because then we will see the growth, the healing, and the gratitude that will fill our hearts will and spur us on to more growth and healing. Praise puts the devil in his place. As I read recently, we are not working *for* Victory, we are working *from* Victory. Christ has already won the battle! Twelve years ago, I couldn't see into the future, but God could. He knew I would be sitting here today writing this story for you to read. Twelve years ago, I sat at this computer (actually it's been replaced a few times through the years), crying my eyes out as I typed the **Me** parts of this book. Today, I sit here with a confident assurance of my salvation, as spoken about in Romans 5:4. How is that possible? Because of Who God is, and no other reason. I have read that gratitude precedes the miracle. That's very true, but it should also follow the miracle!

Do I want it now? YES! I want this pain to go away almost as much as I want Phil back.

I HATED the pain of missing Phil. I HATED missing Phil! I didn't want to go through the grief. I just wanted our son back! But that's just a Mom speaking, and what else would we expect? I still miss Phil every day, but my perspective has changed so much through the years. People look at my husband and me like we are crazy when sometimes we share with them, "We have one son safely Home. It's only the other two we need to be concerned about now." This life is long, and the "terrain" is treacherous. Our other two boys, ages 32 and 35 are married, and they each have three children. Life is busy, and hard, and distracting. They love Jesus, and for that we are grateful. Their wives love Jesus, and their children are learning about Jesus. But it's all still in progress, and there's a lot of hard living to do. Phil rests safely in the arms of Jesus. We know he is greatly blessed!

Do I draw inspiration from women like this? You bet I do!

I have never forgotten the woman who spoke at the retreat I went to. She was about 75 years old, so there's a good possibility that she is now in the arms of Jesus, too. But she left an imprint on my heart for my remaining days on this earth. That is the desire of my heart, that just a little imprint of my story will remain on your heart, and that that imprint would be one of Hope. That is the only reason I am writing this book. There are millions of other stories out there that you could be reading. There are millions who have already walked in my shoes. But maybe you won't come into contact with them, and for whatever reason, you have come into contact with me. Then I must do my part, and tell you about the possibilities there are in grief to grow, and learn, and live again.

With Hope in eternity, this life, with its fleeting problems, diminishes. It can't destroy us!

Remember, we battle not to gain the victory, but from the victory! Life will take us down from time to time, even as Christians. But when we grow, and learn, by spending time in the Word and in prayer, we will start to rebound more quickly after getting knocked down. I read that from a wise pastor, and I have taken it to heart. Too many times we try to be perfect, or we think we should be this way or that as a Christian. The enemy can use our "efforts" to thwart us into thinking we are failing. But as my friend, Linette, once told me, "Even Christians bleed." We are human, made in the image of God. He has given us emotions for a reason. We can use those emotions by working through them, and understanding them. We should not fear them. Fear is of the enemy; it is not of God. Faith is of God. It is a gift. Let's open His gift daily, and enjoy it!

I hope to be able to encourage others and to help them see that Jesus heals the brokenhearted. I hope to come alongside others, share my pain and joy, and show them with God, all things are possible.

Wow, I was getting way ahead of myself there! That truly must have been the Holy Spirit urging me on twelve years ago. But here I am today, writing these very words to you. Thank You, Lord Jesus, for seeing the plans You had for me, for Hope and for a future with You. You didn't mean it for harm, but for my good. Your promises are true. And I love You!

Gift #23 – Seeing God's process working in our lives, and sharing the Good News with others!

What miracles are you witnessing as you take time to look back?

What can you give thanks for on this day, that you never thought would be possible?

Record today's date and other notes you'd like to make:

The Great

I AM

All praise to the God and Father of our Lord Jesus Christ. He is the source of every mercy and the God who comforts us. He comforts us in all our troubles so that we can comfort others. When others are troubled, we will be able to give them the same comfort God has given us.
2 Corinthians 1:3-4 (NLT)

CHAPTER TWENTY-FOUR

In his heart a man plans his course,
but the Lord determines his steps.
Proverbs 16:9 (NIV)

Me

Mother's Day

Saturday, 11 May 2002

How many of you knew I would have to write about this day? I guess most of you expected something, because what day have I missed so far? I mean of the big, important, difficult firsts that we have to go through? Why are the "firsts" always so painful? I wonder why that is, really? It's that way with the small things, too, not just the holidays. The first bowl of clam chowder I ate knowing that Phil loved clam chowder, the first time seeing a movie without him, and even the first haircut I got after he died. They were all very difficult. Was it because Phil didn't know I got it cut? Silly, but true. I don't want anything to change. But it does. I don't want the world to spin. But it does. I don't want to celebrate the holidays. But we do—usually, a bit different than before. Some things being the same, some things being different.

Do you know that Monday will be six months since Phil went Home? I have to say it was the longest winter of my life, so I hope this is the longest summer because I do not look forward to winter again. Although, I know it must come.

Today is a beautiful day here in Pleasanton. Our son, Chris, age 21, and I went out for lunch, his treat to me for Mother's Day. We wanted to avoid the crowds tomorrow in the restaurants. After lunch we took a hike up into the foothills here. It was a warm hike, but very relaxing, as we got the chance to talk as we walked. His life is moving on and he will probably soon be moving out again in with a buddy, some place close. He is ready to be on his own again, and that is fine. I know that God brought him home to be with Phil and us. What a gift that was! God's perfect timing, as he had been in San Diego for almost a year. Can I tell you the story of what brought him home? I think it's a great "God thing." Please bear with me.

Chris was living in San Diego and out looking for work. He had an opportunity to work for a certain company, but he had to join the Union to do so. He needed his birth certificate, his social security card, and his High School transcripts to join. He gave us a call. I gathered those papers together and quickly mailed them to him. But to the wrong address. In the process they were lost! Because that Wednesday had passed, and this could only be done on Wednesdays, we started the process all over again for the next week, also contacting the proper authorities that there might be another "Chris Shore" now walking around San Diego with his papers. So, the next Wednesday came and Chris borrowed a friend's jeep to drive to the Union office. There he was with the papers on the seat next to him, driving down the San Diego freeway when...whooosh! Out of the jeep (convertible) the papers flew! Yes, once again, never to be retrieved because you don't go running around on the San Diego freeways gathering your papers.

Chris called home, once again, to tell us what had happened. He also told me that he felt the need to move home and had been praying about whether he should or not. When the papers flew out of the jeep, for a second, he was frustrated. But then he knew he had his answer. He was not to go after this job, but to head back home. That is when I told him what I had not yet shared with him; that Phil was very sick. I didn't want to tell him that news until after his job hunt was secured. I agreed with him; it was time to move home and to be close to Phil and us. He was packed and moved within the week. What a blessing that was for him to be able to spend those months with Phil.

But, time moves on, and now he is ready to be on his own again. We are ready, too. And in fact, Jimm may be moving back in with us until he secures another apartment in the area. In and out, they come and go. It keeps life interesting!

Speaking of coming and going—my husband, Jim, is off on a motorcycle adventure to Kansas City and back. He met the requirement of riding 1,000 miles in 24 hours, and then another 500 miles within a 36 hour period, so 1,500 in 36 hours. I think this is for a certificate and a pin. Okay! If he calls that fun! He will be back on Tuesday after visiting some relatives in South Dakota. It was a business trip, with adventure, and fun tucked in on each side of it.

Yes, time and life move on, as it should. And holidays come and go, as they should—as Mother's Day will. I know it will be another day that God carries me through, where I try to breathe deep, pray hard, and miss Phil. But I am also so thankful for all that God has blessed me with. The A's play on Sunday, and the weather is going to be sunny and warm. I'll be at the ball park eating a hot dog, same as we did on Resurrection Sunday. That's right! Jim and I went to an A's game on that Sunday, too. That's unheard of for us. But that was another "God-thing." Can I share? This is fun, sharing God things today. You don't have to read this if you don't want to; I'm just enjoying myself here!

Resurrection Sunday, Jim and I are at church, coming out of the service, when my brother, Keith, taps me on the shoulder. There were four large services on Easter, with hundreds of people at each service. But we picked the same service to go to as my brother, and walked out about the same time, not having even known the other was there. We stood in the lobby chatting, and then Keith asked us what we were doing for Easter? We told him we were going to the A's game. Part of me was wondering if God would be angry at us for spending His special day in that way, having never done it before. We had always spent the day with family, but on this day even Jimm and Chris were working, and my sister's family had a terrible flu bug, so we weren't going near their house.

My brother looked at us a bit strangely when we answered his question, and then he said he had two tickets to the A's game for Easter Sunday in his wallet. Did we have our tickets already? Well, no we didn't; we were just going to buy them at the game. He proceeded to tell us that his boss had tickets, in a great spot behind home plate, and had given them to my brother. Keith took them, knowing that he could not use them, because they were going to a brunch. He had just told his wife, during the church service, that the game would be starting soon. He needed to get rid of these tickets, so would we like to have them? Well, you bet we would! Thank you God for this gift! I felt like God had said, go to the game and have a good time on Me. We did!

"God things." They happen all the time. We call them coincidences —or we used to. Now, we call them "God things." To us, nothing is a coincidence. God is in control. We choose our path, but God directs our steps.

It's so much fun to watch God do this. In the past, I could only see this in retrospect. It was like, "Oh, that was God doing that!" But now, I see it happening as it happens. It is fun with God at work! That is why we can rest in Him. He does the work. He just asks us to show up, to trust Him, and allow Him to take care of us. Answered prayers always look different. Chris could have fought against what happened with those papers he lost, gathered them for a third time, and headed back on the next Wednesday to join the Union. He could have. But he didn't. He listened to his heart. Chris listened to God answering His prayers in what seemed a very strange way. But looking back, it was such a wonderful answer. God knew Phil was sick, and He knew Chris needed to be here to spend time with his brother even before Chris knew Phil was sick again. Even before I told him. I didn't want him to plan his life around Phil's illness. Those years had been tough enough on Chris; he needed to do what he needed to do. But God took care of it all, and he brought Chris home with a willing heart. What a blessing!

Just like those A's tickets; we hadn't prayed for free A's tickets behind home plate. But we had prayed for God to help us through that Sunday without Phil. And God did, in a way that only God could do; by blessing us with a gift that shows how much He loves us.

Mother's Day will be no different. I don't know what will happen. Right now, I am not looking forward to it, because I think my heart will hurt more than it normally does. But I can assure you of this, I will have my eyes open, and I will be watching to see what God has in store. I know He's already helping me get through it with the wonderful time he gave me today with Chris. I know that God will be there tomorrow, on Mother's Day, and so will my parents. Their van broke down, and they cannot pull out until Monday. (They travel full time with their trailer.) So, they will be joining me at the A's game. Unplanned in our book, very planned in God's. He will never leave us alone, and most times He will bring others to be with us. (With Jim out of town, and the boys needing to work, it could have been a lonely day.)

Another "God thing?" For sure!

I'll end this with a poem I just wrote. Thanks for "listening" once again.

When Nothing Else Exists

Lord, I know you're with me, I feel You every day
I long to know You better, and as times goes by I stay
Closer to Your presence, soaking up Your Word
I need You close beside me, it's for You alone I thirst
I thought I might not make it, this grief was oh so hard
I missed my precious son, and my heart was torn apart
But You have never left me, each time I call on You
You answer me with kindness, and fill my heart up, too
The hole that was created, when Philip said good-bye
Is filled to overflowing, when I seek You and I cry
Out for all Your strength, to help me when I'm weak
You help me stand and bear it, You never turn Your cheek
And look the other way Lord, when I feel all alone
You are here beside me, with You I am at home
With You I can get comfortable, curl up with Your Book
Dive into its pages, I find You when I look
To You for all the answers, for help in my despair
You're the only One, who is always, always there
You say You are my Savior, I've found that to be true
Not only for Eternity, but in everything I do
I can walk this road Lord, with You here at my side
I can find Your light Lord, in the dark and dreary night
I can stand the pain Lord, that tears my heart apart
Because Your love is bigger, than the hurt this world imparts
I can go on missing, and grieving for my son
But still feel Your joy Lord, when each day is done
Because I know the Hope now, that You have left us with
And I can cling to it, when nothing else exists

Have a Happy Mother's Day!

Love, Diane

<u>Myself</u>

Why are the "firsts" always so painful? I wonder why that is, really?

I should be able to answer that by now. But can I? Let me see... What have I learned about "firsts," and "seconds," and "thirds"? It does seem wrong to just go on living in the beginning. I do remember the first haircut I got. I sat in the chair, with my normal stylist. She spoke broken English, so we didn't converse a whole lot. She asked me how I was doing. I said, "My son died two weeks ago." I know she didn't know if she had heard me right. Then when she realized that she had, she was shocked, and saddened. I don't remember any of the conversation after that. Simple things, like getting a haircut, were no longer simple. Maybe that's what the "firsts" represent, that what *was*, is *no longer*, and it must be faced. But it's SO hard, SO painful! I came home from that haircut, looked in the mirror, and I remember saying, "Phil, you don't know that I got my hair cut today." It seemed wrong to change anything, even little things. And then, to get into the really big stuff, like his bedroom? Everything has to be in God's timing, so that God's "manna" for each day provides enough strength to see us through. So much has changed now, 12 years later. And my hair? It is long, to my shoulders, when it was above my ears last time Phil saw me. It is graying now, and so is Jim's. I smile as I write that. Why? I'm not sure. I think because I am at peace with these changes now. And my heart sees that as a very good thing. Phil would be pleased that I can smile.

Do you know that Monday will be six months since Phil went Home? I have to say it was the longest winter of my life.

The trees were so bare that winter. They looked like my heart felt. I still remember that as the trees drop their leaves each winter. And when the blossoms come back in the spring, like they are right now, I remember the relief I felt. I had made it through that first season, and it felt promising. Spring has always been my favorite season. But for my Grandma it was different. Spring was when she said goodbye, not only to her daughter, but to her husband. Maybe she relished the colors of Autumn? I recently acquired her Bible. Inside the cover she has some old letters. One letter was written to her husband, my Grandpa, just a month before he died. He was gone on a business trip, and was soon to return home. Her cursive handwriting was beautiful, and obviously she loved him very much. She had no idea it would be her last letter to him, but it couldn't have been more endearing. He died, in their home, of a sudden heart attack at the age of 61, when my Dad was eleven. She taught me so much as she went through all the seasons of her life. She showed me life does go on.

Today is a beautiful day here in Pleasanton. Chris (son) and I went out for lunch. His treat to me for Mother's Day.

As God began to heal my heart, I was able to appreciate the sons I still had on this earth. Yes, it took time. As I think about that now, I believe the hard part is loving again. When we love someone deeply, we open our hearts up to be hurt deeply. That is part of the give and take with love. It would be easier when someone dies to just close down our hearts and not love anyone; to protect ourselves from being hurt again. What a travesty that would be. The thing about grief is that it can actually teach us to love better and stronger. Grief can teach us to feel more deeply, to embrace more readily, and even to let go more easily. Many years after Phil went Home, a close friend of mine also joined Phil in Heaven. I remember saying that day, "I gave her my whole heart, and now my whole heart is broken." But what I had learned also in the grieving process is that broken hearts heal. I knew mine would after saying good bye to my friend, even though it hurt terribly in that moment. That was the Hope I learned I had that comes from Jesus. When our eternal life is secure with Jesus, we can live each day with a better focus on all that is transpiring.

Can I tell you the story of what brought him home? I think it's a great "God thing."

It's fun reading this about the "God things," because now I do *The SAND Room* writings about seeing God in each and every day. I truly can see what is happening in the present moment, and give God thanks then and there. It is sort of hard to remember that I used to, most times, have to look back to see God's hand in things. That is encouraging for me, to see that there has been growth through the years. That is God getting us ready to meet Him face to face, to be ready to walk into His Kingdom with full confidence of all that He has promised us in His Word. My friend, Lynn, recently shared a quote with me; it went something like this, "When we put everything into God's hand, we can see God's hand in everything." She couldn't remember who said it, but it was a good one.

Chris called home, once again, to tell us what had happened. He also told me that he felt the need to move home and had been praying about whether he should or not.

I like reading this, all these years later—that Chris, who was about 19 at this time, was praying about what he should be doing. Chris is 33 now. He was so young in his faith at that time. His answer seemed so clear to him when it came, and looking back now we all know it was exactly what he should have done. Those weeks and months with Phil were a precious time that Chris would not have wanted to miss. We all did need to be together as a family.

Phil was very sick. I didn't want to tell him (Chris) that news until after his job hunt was secured.

Everyone's lives are affected when one person's life is affected. We sometimes don't realize the ripple effect we have on others. When there is someone ill in a family, whether that comes from cancer, addictions, mental illness, etc...it affects everyone. Our two older boys had different lives than they would have had because their younger brother was fighting cancer. It meant time away from them as their mom. It meant that their dad was at the hospital each night instead of home. It meant that activities were planned in different ways. We all had to be understanding of the adjustments that were needed, and I'm so thankful as I write this today that we are still a strong family, one that loves the very God who we could have blamed for all of this trouble. We live in a fallen world. Troubles will come, but God is there to see us through, not to be blamed.

I know it will be another day that God carries me through, where I try to breathe deep, pray hard, and miss Phil.

I recently read a book about how the enemy is like a python, squeezing the very air out of our lungs. I read that book 12 years after I experienced that feeling in such an intense way. Even just now, without even thinking about it, I took a deep breath in. I think something in my memory was just triggered as I thought about those times, when even breathing in air was hard because the pain inside seemed to want to keep the air out of my lungs. Grief, stress, tension, heartache, whatever the emotion, it really can and really does affect us physically as well as emotionally. I learned a lot, even while Phil was sick about how my body reacts when stress is present. It is helpful, actually. It helps me know when to say no now, or slow down, or back off just a bit. Those physical aches that can start in my jaw or back when something is going on reminds me it's time to pray, and read the Word. Some turn to alcohol, or drugs, or other things. I understand that; although so many of our choices can be unhealthy. We have to turn to something when times get hard because the pain is so great. Turning to God is our **very best** option. ALWAYS. I saw some writing on a bus just today as I was driving to work. It said, "A healthy conversation is well, healthy." It made me chuckle. It was simple, and made sense. In using that, I say, "A healthy choice is well, healthy."

My brother looked at us a bit strangely when we answered his question, and then he said he had two tickets to the A's game for Easter Sunday in his wallet. Did we have our tickets already?

God is in the details. Yes, times can be hard, but God is bigger than all the hard times we will ever go through. Why did my brother's boss give him two A's tickets? Why did Keith accept them when he knew he couldn't go to the game? Why did we choose to go to the same Easter service, and walk out at exactly the same time? Why, why, why? Because God, God, God—His hand is on all things, at all times, and when we can truly live in the shelter of His wings, we can find rest in His shadow.

Chris listened to God answering His prayers in what seemed a very strange way.

Sometimes God's answers to our prayers can actually frustrate us. Sometimes the answers come too slow, or in ways that we could never imagine, but the answers always come. Now I love looking back when times get tough, and asking myself, "When did God not take care of us?" It reminds me that He always has, and always will. Did we always get what we wanted, when we wanted it? NO! But neither do children, and neither do we as the children of God. Our Father knows what's best, and we have to trust that to be true.

Mother's Day will be no different. I don't know what will happen. Right now, I am not looking forward to it because I think my heart will hurt more than it normally does.

Mother's Day... On this last Mother's Day, just a few weeks ago now, I was amazed at what God had me doing. Eighteen years, to the month, after Phil was first diagnosed with Leukemia, I found myself speaking at a Ladies Tea at First Baptist Church of Cocoa in Florida—talking about the things of God to a large group of women. I NEVER would have thought that would have been possible. It wasn't even in my realm of thinking years ago. I can remember that first Mother's Day without Phil, and my heart hurting all day, and how difficult it was. And now I look back at this last Mother's Day and I see all that God has done. He has brought me through and is allowing me to share His goodness. If you find yourself completely shattered today, hang in there with God. He WILL bring you through. He will do amazing things. And you will be praising Him. I know it's hard to believe; but I urge you to continue to believe!

You say You are my Savior, I've found that to be true
Not only for Eternity, but in everything I do

With Jesus in everything we do, when He is invited into our lives, we will see Him in all things. We will find Him to be our Savior each and every day, and we can look forward to what He has planned. Even on this day, though it may be the worst day of your life, because we all have those days. No one escapes them. But today, we have a Savior that loves us and One who will take care of us. God makes us that promise, and He can be trusted. There are very few "overnight successes" in life. Some may have thought at the tea where I spoke that it was easy for me; but not for them. Perhaps they thought that I had arrived at that place quickly. Let me just say, it was never easy, and it was certainly not quick for me through Phil's illness and then experiencing him going Home to Heaven. There was no overnight success in getting through all that transpired. But the worst days of my life have now brought me to some of the most satisfying days of my life as I await the return of my Savior and the reunion that is to come with my son. It is God's air that I breathe and His Hope that keeps me going each and every day. And the more I depend on my Lord, the more I realize just how dependable He is. I praise You Jesus!

Gift #24 – Seeing the faithfulness of our Savior, Jesus Christ, more and more each day!

Looking back, what's the biggest transformation you have seen in your own life?

Do you attribute this to pulling yourself up by your own bootstraps, or the hand of God pulling you through the muck and the mire?

Record today's date and other notes you'd like to make:

The Great

<u>I AM</u>

I lift up my eyes to the mountains—where does my help come from? My help comes from the Lord, the Maker of heaven and earth.
Psalm 121:1-2 (NIV)

EPILOGUE

If you've come here first—Welcome! If you've just finished reading the entire book first, thank you for taking the time to do that. I truly do appreciate it. I want you to know that everything that I have written in this book is true, to the best of my recollection. I would never have been able to even begin this project 12 years later without all that was written in the early stages of grief. I never could have remembered all the details, and I didn't know then that I would be doing this now. But I am grateful that writing was one of the tools God gave me to work through all the stages of grief. But, this I HAVE TO SAY: None of what I have written here about God's healing power works without the power of Jesus Christ and the Holy Spirit that dwells within each believer. None of it! We all need Jesus to truly live, and to truly heal. This world provides Band-Aids for our hemorrhaging hearts. They may work for a while, but they are not a permanent solution for healing. ONLY GOD IS!

As I finished up with the first six months of what started in the dark of grief, I was a long, long, long way from being set free from the pain and missing that enveloped me. There were moments of joy beginning, there were moments of my heart not hurting, and there were moments of seeing the light at the end of the tunnel. But it took many years for God to accomplish His healing work in my heart. Without the bottom line of the Truth of Jesus Christ, I would not have made it through. And what is the Truth of Jesus Christ? Let me share, in case you are wondering.

Jesus came into this world as a baby, the One and only Son of the living Father God in Heaven. He came to save us. And He did it! After living a perfect, sinless life, He died on the Cross for our sins, rose again from the grave, and ascended into Heaven to sit at the right hand of the Father. Why did He do this? Because we needed Him to. We can't be perfect, although we can try to be good. But good doesn't cut it in God's perfect Home of Heaven. Only spotless records allow us through the Heavenly gates. Jesus said, "Humanly speaking, it is impossible. But with God everything is possible." (Matthew 19:26 NLT) God has made a way for all of us to enter in. It's by the blood of His Son, Jesus. He died, so we can live. He died to conquer sin and death for all of us. His blood washes away the grime of our sinful lives when we choose to repent. Jesus saving grace makes us clean when we stand before the Father in Heaven. Jesus paid the price, so we can receive this free gift of salvation. What an amazing gift! And do you know what comes with that free gift? It's the Holy Spirit, who comes to live inside of everyone and anyone who is willing to receive Jesus Christ as Lord and Savior. Jesus didn't leave us alone when He ascended back into Heaven after His resurrection. His Father sent the Holy Spirit to help us each day until Jesus returns for us. The Holy Spirit guides us, gives us strength, and helps us through each day, no matter what problems or trials we face.

If you have finished reading this book, you have heard a lot about journeying through grief by the power of God. It is available to you by simply surrendering all that you are, to receive all that God wants to give you. God doesn't want us to live hopeless in this hurting world. He wants to give us everything we need to make it through until we are living with Him in Heaven. If you have never said, "Yes" to Jesus, why not today? Jesus said, "I am the way and the truth and the life. No one comes to the Father except through me." (John 14:6 NLT) If you have walls of resistance keeping your heart trapped in pain, and you would like to put your heart at ease, today is the day to be set free in Jesus. Let His process begin!

Pray with me if you will:

Lord in Heaven, I need You. I am lost without You. You came into this world for me, because You love me. You died for me, because You love me. You rose again, because You love me. You ascended back into Heaven to sit at the right hand of the Father and to intercede for me, because You love me. You forgive my sins, because You love me. I want to say, on this day, that I want to love You, too. I want to give You all of me, surrendering to You, turning from my sinful ways, and asking for Your forgiveness. I receive that forgiveness. Thank You for Your Holy Spirit. I look forward to walking out the rest of my days on this earth following You each day, until that day comes when I meet You face to face. Come, Lord Jesus! In Your Holy name I pray. Amen

Thank you for traveling along with me thus far. There's more to come in the book I'm working on right now, entitled "It Ended in the Light." I'm excited to see what God would have me share with you in those pages—it will take us through the last six months of that first year of grief. Grieving takes years, but maybe what I am sharing will help to pour a foundation of Hope in Jesus to build upon. Jesus said, "Therefore everyone who hears these words of mine and puts them into practice is like a wise man who built his house on the rock." (Matthew 7:24 NLT) The foundation of everything we do must be built on the Rock, Jesus Christ.

As we walk these days out together with Jesus as our Savior, we can know, that one day, we will walk eternity out together in Heaven. What a glorious day that will be!

All praise to Jesus Christ my Lord!

Diane

The Gifts We Receive Along The Way.

1. A glimpse of a Heavenly perspective that eases the burdens of this earth.
2. We can start to recognize God's gifts vs. Satan's lies in this world.
3. God's protective fog helps get us through those early days.
4. Discovering the peace Jesus left us with...a peace that surpasses all understanding.
5. Learning to live in the power of the Holy Spirit that is available to all who believe.
6. Rest is okay and even needed. Enjoy the quiet times.
7. Discovering the moment by moment, healing power of our Mighty God.
8. Our priorities can change, and for the better!
9. Understanding that Jesus came to rescue us, and we can help each other, too.
10. None of what we are going through is useless. Our Father has a plan, and we're in it!
11. The very worst in life can point us to the very best there is—Jesus!
12. Realizing a need for a Savior, and finding He is with us, and He works.
13. Knowing that Jesus has provided exactly what we all need!
14. Beginning to see the intricate ways of God working when times are tough.
15. Seeing the Body of Christ working together as it should.
16. Beginning to realize that God's Hope holds so much more for us than this world does.
17. Knowing that we can get through all things, old and new, with the strength of the Holy Spirit, who lives in us.
18. The all-consuming saving knowledge of our Hope in Jesus!
19. Finding God's pain relief is better than anything this world can provide.
20. The Cross of Jesus Christ becoming so real that we are more able to share its Hope with everyone we meet.
21. The gift of more healing when we didn't even realize what needed tending to.
22. Learning to resist the enemy and the forces he brings against us through God's power and protection.
23. Seeing God's process working in our lives, and sharing the Good News with others!
24. Seeing the faithfulness of our Savior, Jesus Christ, more and more each day.

GIVING THANKS

"So the last will be first, and the first will be last."
Matthew 20:16 (NIV)

This may be the hardest page of the book for me to write. Not because I don't have anyone to thank, but because there are so many I would like to acknowledge. Eighteen years ago this journey began at the bedside of our son in Munich, Germany when he was diagnosed with Leukemia. It would take a book just to mention all those who have helped us/me along the way. So, I will limit those I mention on this page to those who have been personally involved in getting this in print. I hope the rest of you will find yourselves somewhere in the stories shared, as you were so much a part of the healing process. It took **all** of you with your prayers, cards, letters, flowers, food, hugs, time spent, listening ears, phone calls, words of encouragement, thoughtful acts of service, etc... No one thing brings a person through something so difficult. But each small kindness helps in its own significant way. So THANK YOU!!

Those who helped to put these pages into book form:

I would not be here today writing this if not for Jesus, my Lord and Savior, the only begotten Son of our Father in Heaven, and the power of the Holy Spirit who lives in me and keeps me going. Lord, You fill me up, and help me pour out Your Hope and Love through my typing fingers.

I would have no way to accomplish all the technical things required without my husband, Jim. No one else would have the patience for the "millimeter" changes I make along the way when we work together on these projects. Jim, you always support me, love me, and encourage me in so many ways!! God has shown me after 38 years of marriage that we are two halves He brought together to make us wholly able to serve Him.
I love you more every day! Thank you for all you do!

I would have laid my "pen" down if not for Connie Dixon, who encouraged me over and over to keep writing. It seemed that enough had been written, but she strongly disagreed. And then, she agreed to edit the things I did write! Not only did you edit what I wrote, Connie, you encouraged me by liking it! And wanting more. I pray God blesses you even more than you have blessed me! Thank you!

Jenn Ackerman, I'm thankful God brought us together through "Closer Coins." The idea for this book came by using these 12-year-old writings to help you when you needed encouragement after your daughter Zeyah Grace entered Heaven. God has used your precious Zeyah to hopefully touch many lives through these pages.

Thank you Debbie Clemmons, for blazing the self-publishing trail for me. In seeing you share Randy's story, "In His Grace, Grappling with Mesothelioma," I was encouraged to do the same.

Thank you to Mockingbird Primitive on etsy.com for handcrafting our window frame that is pictured on the cover. This frame hangs in our home with a poster-sized picture of all our grandchildren displayed in it. I wanted to be able to sit in our living room and always be able to "see" our grandchildren playing "outside." It continually reminds me of Job's blessings, and how God restored his life and ours.

In finishing up the final details of this book, I appreciate all those who helped smooth out any left over rough edges. You are usually the same team that helps me with my own rough edges! Thank you for finding errors, making suggestions, and being bold in your evaluations. Your support, prayers, and encouragement helped to keep this project moving forward when the enemy was pulling out all his tricks to try and stop it. You're all priceless! Thank you!!

Soli Deo Gloria

(To God Alone The Glory)

ABOUT THE AUTHOR
diane.dcshorepublishing.com

Diane C. Shore lives in Danville, California with her husband Jim of 38 years. They have been blessed with three sons, Jimm, Chris, and Phil, and two daughters-in-law, Cami and Holly. They greatly enjoy being the grandparents of Denell, Kylie, Jackson, Maren, Laila, and Cooper. Diane has been using writing as a ministry for many years. As God pours His love into her heart, she pours it out to others in many written forms. She enjoys telling the story of God's Hope and Love through the darkest times. She shares her testimony at churches, and speaks to women at gatherings both large and small. Her favorite thing to do is converse about the things of God, one-on-one, over a cup of coffee.

...he set my feet on a rock
and gave me a firm place to stand.
Psalm 40:2b (NIV)

Photo taken by Aimee D. Harris at Lake Tahoe, CA

To order more copies of *It Started in the Dark* go to:
http://diane.dcshorepublishing.com

It Started in the Dark is also available for Kindle at Amazon

Coming Soon!

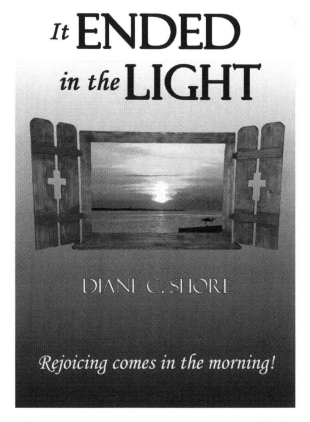

It **ENDED** *in the* **LIGHT**

DIANE C. SHORE

Rejoicing comes in the morning!

It Ended in the Light will be available soon:
http://diane.dcshorepublishing.com

47451323R00148

Made in the USA
Charleston, SC
11 October 2015